Essays in General Psychology

Seven Danish Contributions

Essays in General Psychology

Seven Danish Contributions

presented to Henrik Poulsen

Edited by Niels Engelsted, Lars Hem
and Jens Mammen

AARHUS UNIVERSITY PRESS

Published with the financial support of the
Danish Research Council for the Humanities

AARHUS UNIVERSITY PRESS
Aarhus University
DK-8000 Aarhus C, Denmark

Contents

Introduction   1

Henrik Poulsen (University of Aarhus)
The concept of motive and need in Leontiev's
distinction between activity and action   7

Niels Engelsted (University of Copenhagen)
What is the psyche and how did it get into the world?   13

Boje Katzenelson (University of Aarhus)
The phylogenesis and sociogenesis of the psyche and
the law of correspondence   49

Jens Mammen (University of Aarhus)
The relation between subject and object from the
perspective of activity theory   71

I.K. Moustgaard (University of Copenhagen)
The concept of observation in physics and psychology   95

Ole Dreier (University of Copenhagen)
Private thinking: Towards a theory of therapeutic action
in context   111

Lars Hem (University of Aarhus)
On conations, psychotherapy and the concrete
understanding of persons   133

Henrik Poulsen's published works, 1960 - 1989   145

Introduction

The seven articles to be found in this volume are rewritten versions of lectures that were originally held during a symposium at the Institute of Psychology, University of Aarhus, Denmark, between the 24th and 25th September, 1987. The title of the symposium was "The General Foundation of Psychology" and it was held in order to mark the 60th anniversary of Professor Henrik Poulsen, Dr.Phil.

Several criteria were used to decide whom to invite to speak. One was that the work of the persons concerned had to have been inspired by Henrik Poulsen's activity as a researcher and teacher. Another that they had to be engaged in the field of general psychology and in problems concerning the theoretical and methodological foundations of psychology. It was also required that the lectures should reflect the contemporary developments within Danish psychology, which in some ways are different from the mainstream of academic psychology in the rest of the Western World.

Finally, we decided for practical reasons that the symposium should involve no more than seven lectures, in order to allow time for discussion. Fortunately, many of our colleagues whom it would have been fair to ask to give a lecture, participated eagerly in the discussions. We take this opportunity to thank them.

Danish university psychology has a long tradition for being a psychology of consciousness - an experientially oriented or so-called phenomenological psychology. One can speak of a specific phenomenological Copenhagen-School in psychology: see for example Rubin (1949), Tranekjær Rasmussen (1956), From (1957), and the reviews by Moustgaard & Petersen (1986) and Moustgaard (1987).

During a time when the main part of international psychology has been concerned with man as a biological organism and as an animal amongst animals, with man "seen from the outside" so to speak, Danish psychologists have been true to the humanistic foundations of psychology and have taken as their starting point the specific ways in which man experiences and acts in the world. There is thus a strong tradition within Danish psychology of respecting the enormous wealth of man's experiences. Our training has stressed the necessity of avoiding the conceptual short-cuts offered by various brilliant but too simple theories of man's experiences. This is something we are proud of, a core in our identity as psychologists.

There has, however, also been a more negative side to this tradition. One problem has been a tendency to define the science of psychology in much too comprehensive terms. If psychology is the study of conscious mental life, then everything that one can be conscious of is appropriate subject matter for our science. Absolutely everything in which man takes an interest, including all the other sciences, thus comes under the realm of psychology. In this way psychology strangely comes to encompass everything, and in a way, therefore, nothing. Psychology becomes trivial.

One has fallen into a pit dug by philosophical idealism where the world and the consciousness of it cannot be distinguished from each other.

A classic solution to this problem is to introduce a distinction between the world and the consciousness of it, a distinction based upon the idea that behind the world of which we are conscious lays another world of which we are not conscious. This is the actually existing material world; the world of physics and its invisible atoms. The natural sciences can now occupy itself with this material, but invisible world, while psychology can engage itself in describing and explaining the conscious, experienced world.

Here, however, one found oneself stranded upon an extreme anti-realism, which also is filled with problems. It is impossible on the basis of anti-realism to interpret the data from psychological research as revealing reality, and it is, therefore, difficult to connect practical psychology with academic research.

In many ways this special form of Copenhagen-phenomenology resembles German Gestalt Psychology which it was inspired by, and which it generally in the international literature has been treated as part of. In the Anglo-Saxon literature, German Gestalt psychology has often been treated as a school of psychology opposed to Behaviourism because of their differences concerning the admissability of experiental reports as part of the empirical foundation in a proper scientific psychology. This methodological difference, important as it is, has to a certain extent overshadowed the basic philosophical agreements between the two schools, where the philosophical notions of physicalism and logical positivism have served as the common frame inside which their discussions have been conducted.

Thus, as Schultz (1988) has pointed out, there is a common philosophical foundation for the philosophical idealism of the Copenhagen Phenomenologists and Behaviourism which one was otherwise extremely opposed to. However, there is a paradox in the anti-realism exposed by the Copenhagen Phenomenologists, when they on the one hand asserted that physics is included in the realm of phenomena, and that a notion of objective or material reality was "meaningless", and when they on the other hand claimed that reality, as the cause of phenomena, consisted of in principle uncognisable atoms.

The critique of positivism, as it was turned into a political programme in many universities throughout Europe in the late sixties, thus had a different flavour in Danish psychology than most other places.

These problems and contradictions have in recent years contributed to a widespread awarenes of a crisis within Danish psychology and strong interest in theoretical and philosophical problems, for example manifested as discussions in the journals *Udkast* (1973-) and *Psyke & Logos* (1980-).

This interest in philosophical problem is, however, not a new phenomenon. There has always been a close relationship between Danish philosophy and psychology. One might even say that psychology in Denmark never totally broke away from philosophy. It has also meant that psychologists have used philosophy as a bridge to the fundamental problems of other sciences, e.g. linguistics and physics, which in Denmark also maintained a close connection with philosophy. A focal point for these connections to philosophy is the Danish philosopher Harald Høffding who, at the beginning of the century, inspired the creation of a philosophical study group from which there evolved three "Copenhagen schools": Linguistics, with Louis Hjelmslev as the main driving force; physics, with Niels Bohr as the dominating figure; and psychology with Edgar Rubin as the main spokesman. As pointed out by Christiansen (1985), the threads of these developments can be traced back to Denmark's greatest philosopher Søren Kierkegaard. This is generally recognised in the case of Niels Bohr, but it is less known that similar threads can be traced to a lesser extent within Danish psychology.

A case in point is the classic problems concerning the epistemic relationship between subject and object. As a relationship between observer and the observed, this was a central epistemological theme in Niels Bohr's work, and his reflections have inspired many philosophers and psychologists. It is by no means a coincidence that three of the contributors to this volume (Engelsted, Moustgaard and Mammen) discuss fundamental problems in both physics and psychology, nor that this theme was keenly discussed during the symposium. To name just one of many testimonies to this connection, the 100 year-celebration of Niels Bohr's birth was marked by several Danish articles in the journal *Nordisk Psykologi* (Nordic Psychology) (see Moustgaard, 1986; Nørretranders, 1986; and Andersen, 1987).

This philosophical orientation and the tradition for mutual interest and communication across discipline-boundaries based on it, needs to be taken into consideration if one is to understand the current developments within Danish general psychology. This trend is closely connected with a devotion to problems of general anthropology and of the phylogenetic development of man as is manifested in the papers of Engelsted and Katzenelson.

A characteristic feature strongly reflected in several of the papers in the present collection is the inspiration received over the last ten years from Soviet psychology, partly via German psychology. It is not so much the Pavlovian and physiologically oriented Soviet psychology that has been influential, but rather the trend, starting with Vygotsky, that has found inspiration in Marx's writings. In doing that, the Russians sought the roots of their theorethical conceptualisations in the classical German philosophy which also was the starting point of Danish psychology. This trend in Soviet psychology has in recent times been represented primarily by A.N. Leontiev (see Leontiev, 1978 and 1981). While Marxist psychology in the Anglo-Saxon world mostly has been considered a radical break with the ruling positivistic and pragmatic traditions, in Denmark it has more often been considered a continuation of a native tradition. There are, of course, differences between classical German idealism and dialectical materialism, but there are also many common features in terms of concepts and ways of formulating problems. Regardless of the degree of agreement and acceptance, the texts of Hegel and Marx have not been considered gibberish by Danish psychologists to the same extent as they no doubt have been by many of our colleagues throughout the rest of the world. Neither has there been a dramatic or irreconcilable conflict between Marxist and non-Marxist psychologists in Denmark as there has been in many other countries. We have generally been able to protect academic fellowship and mutual respect - even if voices at times have been loud.

Whether the inspiration comes mainly from Soviet psychology and dialectic materialism, from the social philosophy of western marxism, from the paradigm shift seemingly occurring within the contemporary natural sciences, from the Kierkegaard tradition, or from a combination of these influences, it appears that at present there is a new understanding emerging concerning the relationship between the human subject and his world. On the one hand this new understanding breaks with the idealistic confusion of subject and object, and on the other hand it breaks with mechanistic materialism's contrast of the subject and its world as independent units, externally related. Apparently, there is now emerging a view of the subject-object relationship in terms of practical activity and interdependence.

This also means that the relationship between theory and practice within the science of psychology is being re-evaluated, as is the case for example in Dreier's and Hem's articles in this volume.

It is this current development in Danish general psychology that the publishers of this volume hope to give the reader a taste of. Henrik Poulsen[1] has been a central figure in this development the last couple of decades and we therefore found it appropriate to use the occasion of his 60th anniversary to hold a symposium on the fundamental problems of general psychology.

The publication of this book was made possible by the support of The Humanities' Research Council, The University of Aarhus Research Foundation, The Psychology Faculty Board and the Institute of Psychology, University of Aarhus.
Finally we would like to thank David Glasscock who translated the Danish drafts into English, Henrik Andersen who made the figures, and Lone Hansen who as our secretary kept track of funds, manuscript, notes, etc. and did the word-processing, all with enthusiasm and accuracy.

Lars Hem, Niels Engelsted, Jens Mammen

References

Andersen, S.B. (1987): Niels Bohr's belæringer og psykologiens observations-begreb. (The teachings of Niels Bohr and psychology's observation concept). *Nordisk Psykologi, 39*(3), 203-215.

Christiansen, P.V. (1985): Springet fra København. (The leap from Copenhagen). Feature article in the newspaper: *Information*, 7.10.1985, page 6.

From, F. (1957): *Om oplevelsen af andres adfærd.* (On the experience of others' behaviour). Copenhagen: Nyt Nordisk Forlag, Arnold Busk.

Leontiev, A.N. (1978): *Activity, Consciousness, and Personality.* Englewood Cliffs, N.J.: Prentice-Hall.

Leontiev, A.N. (1981): *Problems of the Development of the Mind.* Moscow: Progress Publishes.

Moustgaard, I.K. (1986): Niels Bohrs tanker om psykologiens observationsbe-greb. (Niels Bohr's thoughts on psychology's observation concept). *Nordisk Psykologi, 38*(1), 27-40.

Moustgaard, I.K. (1987): Dansk eksperimentalpsykologi og dens pionerer. (Danish Experimental Psychology and its Pioneers). In I.K. Moustgaard, J.M. Pedersen & K.H. Teigen (Eds.): *Seculum primum -*

---

[1]   In the back of this book is a list of Henrik Poulsen's published works from 1960 - 1989.

glimt fra 100 års psykologi i Norden. (Seculum primum - Glimpses from a 100 years of Psychology in Scandinavia). Copenhagen: Dansk psykologisk Forlag, pp. 9-18.

Moustgaard, I.K. & Petersen, A.F. (eds.) (1986): *Udviklingslinier i dansk psykologi fra Alfred Lehmann til i dag*. (Developments in Danish Psychology from Alfred Lehmann to Today). Copenhagen: Gyldendal.

Nørretranders, T. (1986): Niels Bohr, subjekt og objekt. (Niels Bohr, subject and object). *Nordisk Psykologi, 38*(1), 65-69.

Rubin, E. (1949): *Experimenta psychologica. Collected Scientific Papers in German, English, and French*. Copenhagen.

Schultz, E. (1988): *Personlighedspsykologi på erkendelsesteoretisk grundlag - eller mysteriet om personen der forsvandt*. (A psychology of personality from the perspective of the theory of knowledge - or the mystery of the person who vanished). Copenhagen: Dansk psykologisk Forlag.

Tranekjær-Rasmussen, E. (1956): *Bevidsthedsliv og erkendelse. Nogle psykologisk-erkendelsesteoretiske betragtninger*. (Conscious mental life and knowledge: Some psychological considerations from a theory of knowledge perspective). Copenhagen: Munksgaard.

Udkast. Dansk tidsskrift for Kritisk Samfundsvidenskab. (Projects. The Danish journal of critical social science). 1973-.

Psyke & Logos. (Psyche & Logos). 1980-.

The Concepts of Motive and Need in Leontiev's Distinction Between Activity and Action

Henrik Poulsen

For some time I have considered Leontiev's concepts of *motives* and *needs* to be problematic, and will here advance a couple of criticisms concerning these concepts. The two concepts form the basis for Leontiev's distinction between *activity* and *action*; a distinction which I would be reluctant to do without. I believe that the destinction can be preserved by a minor modification of Leontiev's concept of action, and for this purpose I will borrow Engelsted's concept of *activities of general utility* (Engelsted, 1989, Vol. 2, p. 265).

To begin with I will briefly outline Leontiev's (Leontiev, 1978, p. 62-63) distinction between activity and action. Every *activity* is said to have an *object*, and this object is the activity's *motive*. To the activity's object and motive there is a corresponding *need*, - the activity's object is the object of a need. *Actions* have *objects* as well. However, actions constitute a special category of activity as their objects are not motives but merely *goals*. The action's object and goal is not the object of a need.

Actions are described as *instrumental activities*. They are activities by means of which one realises those kinds of activities whose objects are motives. For instance, Leontiev (1978, p. 63) characterises the making of fishing tackle as an action, by means of which the person realises the activity of obtaining food. It needs to be underlined that this applies equally to when the tool's maker uses the fishing tackle himself, or if he lets others do the fishing in return for which he receives a share of the catch.

The activity's object is the activity's motive, says Leontiev, but what is to be understood by "the object of an activity"?

When Leontiev himself gives an example of an activity's object, such as in the example with the fishing tackle, he often names food, which the individual seeks to obtain or to consume; but how could one characterise objects of activities in more general terms? In making more explicit Leontiev's concept of activities' objects we are aided by Mammen's discussion of 'motive' and 'object' (Mammen, 1983, p. 207, note 3). Here one finds a distinction between:

- The connection to an object which the subject seeks to realise through his activity, and
- the object which the subject seeks to realise a connection to.

The connection to the object which the subject seeks to realise through his activity is what I will call a *goal*. Examples of this could be the consumption of food, the reading of a book, the building of a bridge, or the climbing of a mountain. The food, the book, the bridge and the mountain are objects which the subject seeks to realise a connection to - they are objects which form part of the activity's goal, and I will call them *goal-objects*.

When Leontiev talks about the objects of activities, it appears that he is usually referring to what I have here called goal-objects, but I can see no reason against also describing the goals of activities as their objects.

The question now is whether these objects of activity, i.e. goal-objects and goals, can be motives of the activities in question. That a goal-object is the activity's motive means, according to Leontiev (1978, p. 62, note 29) that the perception of, memory of or thought of (including the wish for) the goal-object starts or prompts this activity. Leontiev's motive concept is thus a concept of a so-called *incentive*.

The idea of, thought of and wish for an activity's goal must also be able to act as the motive for an activity with this goal. Thus, there is nothing to prevent a person's wish of having built a bridge in a particular place, or the idea of having 'conquered' a particularly difficult mountain, from prompting efforts to build the bridge or attempting to climb the mountain. But this addition to Leontiev's motive concept does not imply any radical changes to the fact that the motive concept is a concept concerning incentives.

Incentive-motivation is found in animals as well as in humans. Thus, for example, the appearance of a predator will be able to motivate an animal to fight or flight. It is, however, criticisable that human motivation should be reduced to a form that is not essentially different to that of animals.

Human motivation encompasses not only incentives which can start activity, but also motives which consist of arguments and reasons for setting oneself the activity-goal concerned. Such *argumentation-motives* can, for example, refer to the relevant activity's effectivity or necessity as a means of bringing about a more distant goal: 'The motive to perform activity a, with the goal g, is that a(g) is suitable for or necessary for the bringing about of the goal g'. An argumentation-motive can also consist of references to moral obligations or customs, etc.

It appears that the difference between an incentive-motive and an argumentation-motive can be expressed in the following way: An incentive merely starts an activity, while an argumentation-motive starts an activity *because it is considered to be a good reason for doing so.*

I have recently seen an excellent illustration of the above in Curt Weibull's book about *Queen Christina* (1969). The book contains a description and study of the motives behind the Swedish queen's abdication in 1654, and her conversion to catholicism. Neither contemporaries of that time nor present day historians have been satisfied with incentives. Both the queen's royal advisors and the historian of today have looked for grounds or reasons for the queen's desire to abdicate. Not only that: They have searched for those reasons which constituted the *real motives*. Some of the queen's reasons were, namely, considered by the royal advisors to be pretexts, and this suspicion was not groundless. The queen could not reveal the decisive motive behind her abdication. She could not tell the royal advisors and the 'Assembly of the Estates of the Realm' that she wished to reject the throne, *because* she wanted to become a catholic, and *because* she considered it to be irresponsible, or against the ideals of "la vertu" (virtue), to remain on the throne as a crypto-catholic.

The queen's wish to convert rested upon more than incentives, it rested upon a solid foundation of criticism against that form of protestantism which she had come to know while growing up in Sweden.

This example illustrates not only that argumentation-motives concern the activity's goal and goal-object, but also that argumentation-motives include other matters as well; e.g. other activities with other goals, moral questions, questions of custom, etc.

With his one-sided attention to incentive-motives and lack of consideration of the fact that human activities, (such as Queen Christina's conversion to catholicism) are based on reasoning and argumentation-motives, Leontiev further overlooks the relevance of argumentation-motives to actions. As mentioned above, Leontiev characterises actions as *instrumental activities*, and as such these activities must be motivated before anything else. They are namely argumentation-motivated by opinions and judgements about their suitability as means of achieving the goals of other activities.

Leontiev's motive concept is too narrow, but broadened by the concept of argumentation-motives it becomes impossible to distinguish between activities and actions on the basis of whether they are motivated or not.

Let us now consider the problems associated with the concept of need.

An activity's object (its goal or goal-object) is said to be the object of a need while the same is not considered to apply to the goal and goal-object of an action.

Leontiev distinguishes between two forms of need (1983, p. 53-54):
- Need as an inner physiological condition for activity and non-directed exploratory behaviour, and

- need that has been transferred from the above named physiological level to the psychological level by becoming object-orientated and thereby capable of directing and regulating the subject's activity in the physical world.

This distinction is reminiscent of the distinction in American psychology between *need* and *drive*; but while the drive concept is more or less one of hypothetical brain processes, Leontiev's concept of object-orientated need concerns mental phenomena, and it is hardly wrong to say that it is a concept of *conations*, that is to say, of striving towards, desiring, hungering for or wishing for something (confer Hem's article in this book).

At the same time Leontiev, like so many other psychologists, overlooks the main meaning of 'need'; i.e. "x being required or necessary for the sake of y" (Nudansk ordborg (Modern Danish Dictionary), 1987, p. 93, 1st column). Thus, he further fails to see the fact that changing social conditions creates totally different needs and as such implicates far more radical changes in the structure of human needs than the replacement of old conation-objects with new ones, as Leontiev suggests (1978, p. 116).

Furthermore, it appears that Leontiev fails to see that needs in the form of conations do not necessarily have to be based on inner physiological states (deprivation states). They may also be based on environmental conditions that can activate the relevant conations in two possible ways: Either in the form of incentives or via the realisation of which needs (by which is meant "x being required or necessary for the sake of y") the environmental conditions in question create. An example of the latter might be that when one's boat fills with water, one comes to realise that it is time to man the pumps.

It strikes me as completely unreasonable to claim that objects of actions are not objects of needs when one considers how Leontiev exemplifies actions. Leontiev (1978, p. 63) gives as an example of an action the making of fishing tackle which the person either uses for fishing himself or lets someone else use in return for a share of the catch. This example is in fact a fine illustration of the production of an object which the person *has a need for* (has a requirement for) either as something he can directly use or more indirectly exchange for something else. At the same time there is no doubt that both the manufacture of the fishing tackle and the acquirement of food have been objects of the person's needs qua conations.

One cannot characterise actions as instrumental activities while at the same time describing them as activities whose goals are not objects of needs.

But neither can Leontiev's definition of actions, based on a narrower concept of life-supporting needs (preferably organically based), be maintained. On the one hand he characterises (in connection with his example of an action) the procurement of food by fishing or exchange as an activity despite the fact that the life-supporting need is not directly satisfied by food procurement (the food still needs to be cooked and prepared), while on the other hand he describes the production of fishing tackle as an action, despite the fact that the activity's purpose is to enable the satisfaction of a life-supporting need.

The only difference is that the procurement of food is a small step closer to the satisfaction of the life-supporting need than the production of the fishing tackle. But how close to the satisfaction of a life-supporting need do we have to come before an action turns into an activity? And why is the borderline placed where it is?

Leontiev has failed to establish a satisfactory criterion for the distinction between activities and actions on the basis of whether or not an activity's object is the object of a need. Furthermore, and as stated above, the motivation criterion is also problematical as a basis for this distinction.

Despite this, it appears to me that something supportable remains at the heart of both the distinction between activities and actions and in the idea that the goal of an action is not the object of a need. This distinction and idea can be made tenable if we interpret the action concept as being equal to Engelsted's concept of activities of general utility. (Engelsted, 1989, Vol. 2, p. 265 and onwards).

It is by no means unreasonable to believe that through his concept of actions Leontiev has attempted to come to terms with a form of activity which we are so familiar with from our everyday lives.

For example, this form of activity includes fishing by commercial fishermen, the professional bricklayer's building of houses, the hairdresser's cutting of hair, etc. The fisherman does not fish because he wants fish for dinner as often as possible, the bricklayer does not build houses for himself, and the hairdresser does not cut hair because he cannot bare to see long-haired people.

The crucial element in deciding if an activity is an action is not whether or not the activity is instrumental. Actions are activities whose goals or goal-objects are brought about because *other* people require or desire these activities' objects. The fisherman catches fish, the baker bakes bread, and the bricklayer builds houses, because there is a need and demand in the general population for fish, bread and houses. This does not mean, however, that actions cannot at the same time be based on the individual's own needs or wishes. The action concept is not one of altruism.

Activities that do not fall within the bounds of the action concept are *not* based on others' needs of or wishes for the relevant activity-objects. These activities may be based on need for the activity-objects concerned but in this case it is the individual subject's own need which is relevant. The subject's wish to bring about a given activity's goal can (as stated above) act as an incentive, but the wish cannot be the reason for this activity - it cannot be an argumentation-motive.

A consequence of this way of drawing the distinction between activities and actions is that activities (outside of the bounds of the action concept) may very well be instrumental in relation to actions, whereas Leontiev only considered the possibility of actions being instrumental in relation to activities. Let me illustrate this relationship with the case of a fisherman who;
- makes ready his boat,
- repairs his nets, and thereafter
- goes to sea after fish.

The first two preparatory activities are not actions; The fisherman makes his boat ready because *he* requires it in order to go to sea, and he repairs his nets because *he* requires them to fish with. But the actual fishing with which the sequence of activities ends is an action: The fish are needed and valued by others. If the fisherman did not believe this he probably would not catch them. For the fisherman the fish have only exchange value.

I will summarise what has been said in the following points;
- As a concept of incentive-motives, Leontiev's motive concept is too narrow. It does not include the argumentation-motives, which are of major importance with respect to human activities.
- Leontiev's denial of the possibility that actions can be need-based and motivated is untenable and thus inadequate as the basis of his distinction between activities and actions.
- It is suggested that the heart of Leontiev's action concept can be saved and made tenable by defining actions as that type of activity whose object (goal or goal-object) is brought about because other people have a need or wish for these activity-objects.

References

Engelsted, N. (1989). *Personlighedens almene grundlag*. (The general foundation of personality). Aarhus: Aarhus University Press.

Leontiev, A.N. (1978). *Activity, consciousness, and personality*. Englewood Cliffs, N.J.: Prentice-Hall.

Mammen, J. (1983). *Den menneskelige sans*. (The human sense). Copenhagen: Dansk Psykologisk Forlag.

Nudansk ordbog. (Modern Danish Dictionary) (1987). Copenhagen: Politikens Forlag (13th edition).

Weibull, C. (1969). *Dronning Christina* (Queen Christina). Copenhagen: Fremad.

What is the psyche and how did it get into the world?

Niels Engelsted

The question

In this paper I will discuss what is for psychology the most fundamental of questions, namely, *what is the psyche?*[1] This is a question which Henrik Poulsen has been especially interested in, and which he and I have had a discussion about for years. This paper then is also a contribution to our ongoing discussion.

The problem

The central theme of the discussion can be presented best by quoting Aristotle who writes in *De Anima*: "Animate nature is thought to be different from the inanimate in two particulars, viz. in movement and sense-perception. And these, I may say, are the two traditional characteristics of the soul which we have received from earlier writers."[2]

Where there are two alternative characteristics, there arise two camps, each with its own viewpoint. In this case, one camp that holds "the view that the soul is a self-moving entity"[3], and another camp that chooses, with respect to the psyche, to "emphasise the knowledge and perception of reality."[4]

Although our point of departure has been the Russian psychologist A.N. Leontiev and not thinkers of Antiquity, these were the positions that Henrik Poulsen and I had placed ourselves in. I stressed Leontiev's keyconcept of *activity* and emphasised the psychic as something conative, whereas Henrik Poulsen stressed Leontiev's keyconcept *reflection* and emphasised the psychic as something cognitive. The following quotation from Henrik Poulsen's article,

---

[1] The terms psyche and psychic in this article refers to the most simple and basic relation studied by the science of psychology. The terms mind and mental denotes according to the author's point of view a higher development of the psychic faculties and should be distinguished from the basic relation.

[2] Aristotle: De Anima, 404a 2. Cf. Hammond, 1902, p. 10.

[3] Aristotle: De Anima, 406a 1. Ibid., p. 18.

[4] Aristotle: De Anima, 404b 10. Ibid., p. 13.

"Leontiev, genspejlingsbegrebet og den almene psykologi" (Leontiev, the concept of reflectivity and general psychology) from 1982 states the case:

> The concepts of reflectivity and activity are (as they must necessarily be) closely coupled together in Leontiev's theory. But it is reflectivity (cognition) and not activity that Leontiev has defined as psychology's object of study. This has troubled some of his readers, e.g. Engelsted, who would have preferred it if Leontiev had denoted man's conation, his striving, his actions, his activity as the object of psychological study. In my view though, Leontiev's judgement is correct.

The problem's special character is also illustrated by the fact that we both became convinced that the other was right. Thus, Henrik Poulsen shifted the emphasis in his position from the cognitive to the conative, as can be seen for example, from his important article on conations (Poulsen, 1986). Correspondingly, I realised the extent to which cognition and mentality are inextricably bound up with each other, and the argument could continue.

The legacy of modern psychology

The conflict concerning cognitive versus conative determination of mentality is a fundamental part of the legacy of modern psychology. If Wundt's establishment of the Psychophysics Laboratory in Leipzig in 1879 marks the birth of scientific psychology, then his two volumed work *Grundzüge der Physiologischen Psychologie* from 1873-74 marks the act of procreation. But in that case psychology had two fathers, for between Wundt's two volumes Brentano shipped in *Psychologie vom empirischen Standpunkte*. Thus the child acquired a split personality. For while Wundt emphasised the analysis of the cognitive content as psychology's task, Brentano emphasised the study of conative acts. If we also take into consideration the third claimant for paternity, the Russian physiologist Sechenov with his publication *Who must investigate the problems of psychology and how?* - also from 1873, then we have the principled positions that have been recurrent in psychology's development right up to today.

One can see that what is involved is a continuation of the fundamental philosophical problem of the simultaneous separation and connection of that which is subjective and that which is objective, which runs like a leitmotif through the whole of philosophy's history. Brentano, who is directly inspired by Aristotle, maintains the classical idealistic viewpoint that sees the subject (the psychic element) as actively determining the objective element (S => O), while Wundt and Sechenov maintain the classical materialistic viewpoint that sees the subject as being determined by the object (O => S). The difference between Wundt and Sechenov is that while the latter chooses to view the psyche from the outside, e.g. as something objective, the former chooses to view it from the inside, e.g. as something subjective.

It is not difficult to see that this is the kind of problem in which all parties possess a truth. The subjective and objective aspects need to be comprehended in one context, where the subjective aspect is simultaneously both determining and determined; where the mind or psyche is simultaneously both conative, as Brentano rightly claims, and cognitive, as Wundt rightly claims; and where Sechenov is also correct in asserting that the psyche must be understood as a fact in the objective, physical world and not as a world apart.

On the other hand, it is more difficult to find the solution that can make room for these different truths. It is, however, such a solution one is looking for when one asks - what actually is the psyche?

Psychogenesis

If one acknowledges that the psyche is a qualitatively new type of relation in the world, and that like other qualitatively different material relations (nuclear, atomic, chemical, biological, etc.), it is a product of the evolution of matter, then the question of what the psyche is can be tied together with the question of how the psyche came into the world?

In *Principles of Psychology* from 1855 Herbert Spencer expresses this insight by saying, "mind can be understood by showing how mind has evolved". Sechenov says the same with these words: "Scientific psychology and all its contents cannot be anything else than a series of teachings about the origin of psychic activity" (cf. Leontiev, 1978, p. 57).

With respect to our question, however, it is very important that a distinction is made between *evolution* and *origin*. One can study different specific mental manifestations, e.g. emotions, by examining the evolution of the psyche. But we ask: What is this psyche that evolves? Or what is psyche in general? To answer this question we must look at the first origin of the psyche in a world where there was not previously anything psychic. For as Klaus Holzkamp (Braun et al., 1983, p. 134) says, *"the earliest genetic form* must also be the most *general category"*. This last point may be surprising, but it is very important to understand that the birth of the first member is also the birth of the whole category. A vast development separates the Wright brothers' first prototype from a modern Boeing 707, but the latter is no more an aeroplane than the former, the former no less than the latter. A molecule of protein is a world of complexity compared to a simple molecule of hydrogen, but still they share the essential nature of a molecule, i.e. the bond between electrons. In the same way, the mind of man may be eons away from the first psychic manifestations in the organic world, but still they must share the essential characteristics of psyche in general. Through all its specific evolutionary developments psyche remains what it was in the very first instance. This is the key to understanding what psyche is.

Continuity and discontinuity

This means that our own psyche's most general feature is a key to understanding what psyche is, and hence, to what the first psychic manifestation was. Not only is it possible, it is also necessary to infer from our own psychic experience to the most simple form of psychic life. If, for example, we are convinced that striving or conation is a general and essential aspect of our psychic life, we cannot deny simple psychic forms this aspect.

This concept does not invalidate Lloyd Morgan's Canon which forbids us to credit lower life forms with properties other than those that are necessary to explain their life-activity. It is an important methodological rule aimed at countering our tendency towards anthropomorphism, e.g. Darwin's attributing dogs with spiritual tendencies (Darwin, 1889, p. 95). It is also relevant in our present context where we view it as a demand for a precise distinction between the general and specific characteristics of psyche. Darwin's mistake was his generosity in letting the dog partake in specific human characteristics.

Darwin's lack of recognition of the psychic discontinuity between dog and man was, interestingly enough, due to his correct acknowledgement of the psychic continuity throughout the whole animal kingdom. Darwin namely believed that the one excluded the other. We will not complain, however, about his one-sidedness. It was the one-sided view of continuity (the classical canon *Natura non facit saltum*[5] and the geological *uniformitarism*) that aided in the birth of evolutionary theory.

Evolution, however, is always a unity of continuity and discontinuity; that which evolves simultaneously changes and remains. The psyche is the same as it has always been (continuity), according to the rule about the identity between the first and the general. And at the same time it evolves a sequence of qualitatively distinct levels (discontinuity) that, as Lloyd Morgan's Canon states, must not be mixed together. The two rules are therefore simultaneously applicable, and if they are contradictory then it is because development is essentially contradictory.

With the exception of some brilliant glimpses by a few individuals such as Heraclitos and Hegel, the dialectical synthesis of continuity and discontinuity, and thereby the conceptualisation of true development, has been beyond the reach of scientific thought prior to the advent of dialectical materialism. This has resulted in discontinuity being stressed at the expense of conti-

---

[5]   Nature makes no leap.

nuity, or continuity being stressed at the expense of discontinuity - with endless ensuing battles.

The conceptualisation of psyche requires the simultaneous presence of both continuity and discontinuity; or, expressed in evolutionary terms: Mentality is simultaneously both a continuation of the physical world with which it is congruous, and the expression of a qualitatively different non-reducible principle. Both parts are necessary since psyche is true to the physical world as well as to itself.

Sharing their common world, however, never seemed to be an easy matter for the psychic and the physical. At least not if you judge from the battle of the sciences.

Change of guard

The paradigm shift from Aristotelian to Galileian thought that occurred around year 1600, and which we connect with the birth of the modern natural sciences, could, of course, only be accepted by the natural historians with difficulty. One was willing to accept that falling stones and orbiting planets could be better explained in terms of external mechanical forces, but the concept of teleological[6] striving was still held to be valid for living forms.

Thus the English natural historian John Ray protested against the natural sciences' replacement of the old teleological explanatory principles with new mechanical ones, and wrote that "these mechanic philosophers being in no way able to give account thereof from the necessary Motion of Matter, unguided by Mind of Ends, prudently therefore break off their system, when they should come to animals" (Ray, 1701, p. 48.).

Naturally he should not have done this. His colleague in the newly founded *Royal Society*, the physicist and chemist Robert Boyle, who was England's leading advocate for introducing the new mechanical explanatory system in science, replied that he "that knows the structure and other mechanical affections of a watch, will be able by them to explicate the phaenomena of it, without supposing that it has a soul or life to be the internal principle of its notions or operations." "While he who does not understand the mechanics of a watch may believe as those of China did when the Jesuits first brought watches

---

[6] The term teleological is used in this paper to denote descriptions or explanations in which notions concerning an intention form a part, that is, where events or acts of behaviour are carried out with reference to some future situation, goal or end; i.e. where the nature of the end in some sense and degree plays a part in determining or governing the course of those events or acts of behaviour. In contrast, mechanical explanations refer here to the opposite, i.e. events and behaviours which are determined according to some past or present situation. This distinction is in line with the two different types of causality named by Aristotle as causa finalis and causa efficiens, respectively.

thither, that a watch is an European animal, or living body, and endowed with a soul" (Cf. Le van Baumer, 1978, p. 315). Which implies that when Ray believes that a psyche or a teleological principle is necessary in any explanation of a living organism, it is because in his ignorance he has not grasped that a living creature is completely explainable in the same way as the watch is - in terms of mechanical motion between the elements that the organism is composed of.

Thus, the living organism became a machine, in which the mental aspect, in the words of the French doctor and materialist LaMettrie (1748), is merely a question of "a few more wheels, a few more springs", for as he further writes - "all the faculties of the soul depend to such a degree on the proper organisation of the brain and of the whole body that apparently they are but this organisation itself".

It is to their credit that the natural historians did not give up. To deny the living organism's purposive striving was to deny the evident. If the organism was a mechanical machine, then there at least resided a special life-force[7] in it, which was not to be found in inanimate forms.

That mechanism breeds vitalism is inevitable. One half-truth must call forth the denied opposite half-truth with a vengeance. The conflict can only be settled by bringing the realities and the interconnection of the objective and the subjective together in a unifying theory, and this is only possible with an evolutionary theory. Such a theory has in effect been formulated by the brilliant natural scientist Jean Baptiste Lamarck at the end of the 18th and the beginning of the 19th century. It drowned, however, in the counter revolutionary events in France and has since been grotesquely misrepresented. The whims of history thus denied the coming scientific psychology a very ideal starting point, and it had to set off from the more primitive problem defined by the conflict of mechanism and vitalism.

The pact of the four students

One of the founding fathers of experimental physiology was Johannes Müller in Berlin, who's name is tied to the discovery of the specific forms of sensory energy, e.g. the fact that the quality of sense perception (i.e. sound or light) is dependent on the stimulated nerve and not the nature of the stimulus. Consistent with the vitalistic tendency of German Romanticism Müller referred this to spiritual forces in the body which so upset four brilliant students of his that

---

[7] This life-force has in the course of time had many names, e.g. the entelechia of Aristotle, the pneuma of Galenos, the archeus of Paracelsus, the moule interne of Buffon, the vis essentialis of Wolff, the Lebenskraft of Johannes Müller, and later the élan vital of Bergson and the entelechi or psychoid of Driesch.

they formed a pact in 1845 swearing never to budge from the conviction that "no other forces than common physical chemical ones are active within the organism" (Boring, 1950, p. 708).

The four students were von Helmholtz, du Bois-Reymond, Carl Ludwig, and Ernst Brücke, and their students were the founders of scientific psychology. Wundt studied with Müller, next with von Helmholtz and du Bois-Reymond. Sechenov studied with Müller, and then with du Bois-Reymond and Carl Ludwig. Ernst Brücke had a no less famous pupil, young Sigmund Freud in Vienna. In this way the pact itself became the point of departure for scientific psychology, the task of which became the conceptualisation of psychological phenomena without reference to vitalistic or spiritual forces, i.e. forces of a non-physical nature.

This programme is still valid. If we are to answer the question of what psyche is, we must strictly adhere to the letter and spirit of the pact.

This does not mean that psyche is *nothing but* the principles generated by physiology. Psyche is a set of principles in its own right and cannot - despite Sechenov's brave efforts - be reduced to physical principles as studied by physiology.

The timeless identification of psyche

What is it then that sets psychic phenomena apart from physical ones? It is the contention of this paper that this has basically been known through all history. Only the conceptual systems have varied according to ideology and scientific insight, i.e. to the productive relations and productive forces. The essence of the psyche cannot be unknown to reflecting mental beings such as ourselves. It is precisely the phenomena of cognition and conation as Aristotle wrote in the first treatise on the psyche.

In the chapter in *Psychologie vom empirischen Standpunkte* dealing with the difference between that which is psychic and that which is physical Brentano points precisely to Aristotle and writes: "In his treatise on the soul he says that that which is sensed as such is in him who senses; that the sense (mind, psyche) registers that which is sensed without (its underlaying) matter ...." (Brentano, 1874). Thus, Brentano emphasises the ideal character of cognitions. The form of the material object is reflected by the knower in an ideal form (where the object exists without really existing), and this dual existence of the object (as material and ideal entity) is cognition.

Ideality as content is, however, insufficient as a definition of mentality. According to Brentano the psychic aspect is fundamentally an act: "Every psychic phenomenon is characterised by that which the Scholastics of the Middle

Ages have called the intentional (or mental) inexistence[8] of an object, and which we, in somewhat ambiguous terms would call the reference to a content, the direction toward an object ..., or an immanent objectivity. Every (psychic phenomenon) contains something as its object, but not every psychic phenomenon does so in the same manner. In presentation, something is presented; in judgement, something is affirmed or denied; in love, something is loved; in desire, something is desired and so on" (ibid.).

With these concepts Brentano emphasises the anticipatory nature of that which is psychic. Immanent objectivity or intentional inexistence implies that the object must ideally exist in the act before it can be brought into existence. What is meant is an orientation towards an object in the world, a future goal, i.e. a purposive act.

This fusion of the cognitive and conative (striving) elements in an intentional anticipation is the essence of the psyche. Brentano writes: "This intentional inexistence is exclusively characteristic of mental phenomena. No physical phenomenon manifests anything similar. Thus, we can define mental phenomena by saying that they are such phenomena as include an object intentionally within themselves" (ibid.).

The Soviet psychologists Davydov and Zinchenko attest to this with the following quotation from an anonymous classic source "about the nature of the mind (soul) that gets to the very essence of the problem", as they put it. The quotation reads: "If you do not know what you are looking for, then why are you looking; if you know what you are looking for, then why are you looking for it?".

Davydov and Zinchenko continue: "This fundamental contradiction is the true source of the development of the mind of animals and man. Psychology as a science itself develops by advancing the development of concepts that enable it, in one way or another, to reveal the possibility of resolving this contradiction. To look for something that does not yet exist but that is possible and is presented to the subject only as a goal, something that exists as an idea and is not yet actual: this is the fundamental, cardinal aspect of the vital activity of every sentient being - a subject" (Davydov & Zinchenko, 1981, p. 24).

We change Brentano's, Davydov's and Zinchenko's words into our own. The intentional inexistence of the object in the activity of the subject is the general characteristic of the psyche in all its forms, i.e. also in the very first form. This is the same as saying that that which is psychic is a teleological principle (cf note 6). Psyche and teleology refer quite simply to the same thing.

---

[8]   The term inexistence here has the double meaning of material non-existence of the object in the mental act and yet the object's actual existence in the intention, NE.

To explain how this phenomenon arrives in the world without offending the pact of four is the fundamental task of defining the psyche.

The decisive importance of an evolutionary theory

The fact of the psyche was not unrecognised by the pioneering physiologists. It is not without cause that psychology was spawned from their work and teaching. Müller's bright students probably never felt sure that the old man's famous dictum - *Nemo psychologus nisi physiologus*[9] - might not read equally well both ways. When they rejected the helping hand of vitalism, and herein lay their scientific significance, it was impossible for them at the same time to bridge the principles of physics and physiology and the fact of psychic phenomena. They had understood that if one was not able to explain mentality on the materialistic basis of physics and chemistry, then one could not explain it at all. But at the same time it appeared so hopelessly impossible to acknowledge that which is psychic as a genuine, irreducible principle, that du Bois-Reymond in his *Seven Riddles of the World* from 1882 counted it as one of the seven (in effect three of the seven) fundamental enigmas which science had to give up on. Sechenov's resolute reductionism and Wundt's lame psychophysical parallelism did not disprove this point.

The problem was then a dialectical one concerning the simultaneous connection and separation of that which is subjective and that which is objective, which is only comprehensible with a theory of development. The pioneers did not possess such a theory and the problem of the psyche was therefore an unsolvable puzzle. Darwin's theory, when it eventually arrived, was not of much help either. All things considered, a theory of natural selection is not a theory of development.

There is therefore, not least because of this, reason to regret that Lamarck's work was so unrecognised. Half a century before the pact of four he had formulated precisely the same rejection of vitalism: "The laws that rule all those mutations we observe in nature are always the same and never in mutual contradiction; yet they produce in the living bodies results which are vastly different from those occasioned in the bodies lacking life and which are their opposite altogether." Or, put another way, it is the same laws, e.g. the known physical laws, which apply to living as well as non-living bodies. Thus, no "arché-vitale" or vitalistic principle of life exists. This is so, even though the living follows a completely opposite principle to the non-living (Lamarck, 1830, vol. 2, p. 91-94).

Lamarck talks here of the living and not of the psychic. It is very important to distinguish between these two, but for Lamarck the problem of life and the

---

[9]   No psychologist who is not a physiologist.

problem of the psyche were interconnected, as they have been for most bio-logical theorists from Aristotle to today. This, as such, is not a false idea, the comprehension of the psyche is inseparable from the comprehension of life and its development.

One of the world's mysteries that according to du Bois-Reymond fell be-yond the reach of science was the origins of life. But it was not an impossible problem for Lamarck. The Jacobine revolution in 1793 had presented a pro-fessorship in invertebrate zoology to the 50 year old botanist from the Royal Gardens, and his classificatory labours in this huge virgin territory forced the concept of evolution upon him. Lamarck worked with this problem on what was according to the conditions of the time, a truly scientific basis until his death in 1829. The counter-revolution subdued his work, but could not halt the old man.

The interconnection of the sciences

Lamarck had understood the very principle of development, i.e. the simul-taneity of discontinuity and continuity. A new stage in the development of matter represents its own unique features, but at the same time it is born from the principles of the preceding stage and cannot be in violation of these principles. Life is qualitatively different from chemistry and physics, but it must be brought into existence by the forces of chemistry and physics.

The same applies for the subject matter of the other natural sciences. The laws of chemistry, for example, are the special characteristics of the molecular bond between electrons in atoms. Chemistry as a science *pre-supposes* the existence of this relation and cannot therefore explain how it came into being. Only the science studying the preceding level of material or-ganisation can do this, i.e. the science studying the principles of atoms. The au-tonomy and interconnectedness of the sciences thus reflect the discontinuity and continuity of material development.

This is also the case with psychology, who's object - the psyche - is a completely new quality in the world. The laws of this new quality can and should be studied by psychology, but psychology cannot itself (e.g. within its own subject area) explain how the psyche as a new quality came into being.

If we undertake for the sake of illustration the traditional Cartesian division and talk about the physical principle and the psychic principle, then it will tell us that the coming into being of psychology's object occurs in physic's subject area and in accordance with the laws of the physical world.

Here we have in addition the simple reason as to why psychology has had so much difficulty in - not understanding - but conceiving that which is psychic; namely, the immaturity of physics, and not psychology, as a science. For as long as physics has not cultivated the ground from which the psyche, as a new quality, shoots up, the conceptualisation (but not the description) of that which is psychic has been beyond the reach of psychology. For as long as physics is only able to model the permutations of complex, macroscopic matter as the workings of simple machines, the psyche must haunt the premises as a ghost.

Lamarck's modern insight

Lamarck understood this and in the formulation of the qualitative difference between animate and inanimate matter he is strikingly modern. Lamarck points out that the fundamental tendency in inanimate matter is that which William Thomson formulated half a century later as the second law of thermo-dynamics[10], which states that growing *entropy* is the law of time. In contrast, the characteristic tendency of animate matter is that the processes involved result in higher organisation and greater complexity, i.e. travel in a negative entropic direction (Lamarck, op.cit.).

Does this mean that that which is living falls beyond the laws of physics? Yes, in the sense that living matter travels counter to the natural direction of thermodynamics. But this happens only by virtue of the same physical laws. And if this sounds contradictory, then it is no more so than the fact that the sailing boats in the Bay of Aarhus are able to beat to windward, but only by virtue of the wind.

In any case, Lamarck maintains in this contrast the principle of materialism in that he says, "every fact or phenomenon observed in a living body is, at one and the same time, a physical fact or phenomenon and a product of organisation" (Lamarck, 1815-22). But organisation is something other and more than LaMettrie's mechanical composition; the secret of life must be sought in a special context or process. The living body is "toujours actif", and it is in the *organised activity* that we will find life's distinctive feature. Today this is a fashionable acknowledgement. During Lamarck's time, where living organisms were explained as spirits or watches, it was, of course, far ahead of its time. Take, for example, Lamarck's description of how life, as a special form of material organisation, could spontaneously arise by virtue of known physical laws and the effect of common physical agents. Here he mentions "l'air atmosphérique, différenz gaz, l'eau, [....] le calorique, l'électricité" (Lamarck, 1830, p. 85) and asks "why should not heat and electricity act on certain matters under favourable conditions and circumstances?" (Lamarck, 1802).

Why not indeed? A decisive breakthrough for science on the matter of the beginning of life was, of course, Stanley Miller's experiment in 1952 which

---

[10] The first law of thermodynamics - the law of the constancy of energy - was formulated by von Helmholtz in 1847, i.e. as a direct continuation of the pact of four.

23

demonstrated that organismic macromolecular structures which are the prerequisite for life, could be spontaneously formed when electric sparks are sent through a water-based solution of ammonia, methane and hydrogen; i.e. under experimental conditions designed to correspond to the conditions on our planet in its infancy. This - and later studies that used other substance combinations and sources of energy - can be seen as the experimental affirmation of Lamarck's hypothesis, that "by means of heat, light, electricity and humidity nature forms spontaneous or immediate generations at the extreme of each realm of living bodies where the simplest of bodies are to be found" (Lamarck, 1830, p. 80).

What is life?

The spontaneous self-organising ability of nature which Lamarck drew attention to, is the big breakthrough area in modern physics, which has consequently, on the basis of thermodynamics, cybernetics, information theory, bio-chemistry and ecology, and through conceptions such as Prigogine's dissipative structures[11], Eigen's hypercycle and Mandelbrot's chaos - to name but a few - brought complex material organisation, and thereby life, within the secure reach of science.

But at the same time as modern macroscopic physics begins to offer physical principles for the comprehension of the preconditions of life, the problem of distinguishing between these principles and life in itself arises as a specific problem. Life is spontaneous material self-organisation, as Lamarck saw, but self-organisation in itself is not life. Non-living material systems share this ability to establish order against entropy when they receive and dissipate energy, as Prigogine has recently demonstrated, and as Schrödinger already pointed out in the famous treatise *What is Life?* in 1944. In the same way life is without exception a self-replicative phenomenon, but replication in itself is not life. Many non-living material systems replicate. The shadow of the central dogma, however, here seems to obscure our understanding of life.

The physicist Freeman Dyson has specifically tackled this problem in *Origin of Life* from 1985. In his critique of Schrödinger and others he insists upon the distinction between replication and metabolism, and suggests that life has had two beginnings. First in the form of metabolism and hereafter as metabolism and replication, in that cells with metabolism have entered into a symbiosis with replicative structures. In support of this view, Dyson states that there actually exist forms of matter that possess the property of genetic replication without metabolism, namely viruses, which as is well known live as parasites on other living cells. And there are probably also forms of life that

---

[11] See Jens Mammen's paper in this volume.

possess the property of metabolism without genetic replication, namely, the so-called prions which cause disease in sheep and supposedly are proteins without nucleic acid.

By accounting life's first beginning to metabolism Dyson has also made metabolism the defining feature of life. In this I believe him to be right (Engelsted, 1981, p. 105-112), but the essential characteristic of metabolism can be given a more general formulation.

The principle of life

The precondition for spontaneous self-organisation is the inflow of energy. That which distinguishes living systems from non-living ones is the fact that the former control this inflow. In their first Oparin-like forms they are monads, but monads with windows and like Maxwell's demon they can open and close these windows. This self-active moment distinguishes metabolism (and thus life) from mere exchange.

In a philosophical sense the living system thus is a subject, as biological thinkers since Aristotle have acknowledged. But this does not go beyond the facts of physics, and only means that the living system has access to its own sources of energy, which, of course, all known living forms from bacteria to man have in the form of cellular ATP.

The expenditure of energy as the precondition for the intake of energy - food - is the defining characteristic of life. Life must break down its own order to be able to build up its own order. (Of course, the investment must be profitable for life to succeed.) Life is thus a realisation of the general thermo-dynamic principles where dissipation of order makes possible the opposite negative entropic movement. But it is a particular realisation, and the particularity is the subjectness of the living system.

The definition is not, however, hereby complete. Just as a subject cannot be comprehended in isolation from its object, a living organism cannot be comprehended in isolation from its external sources of energy. If life is the ability to feed through the expenditure of its own energy on an external stream of energy, one cannot exclude the latter part from the definition. One cannot exclude sugar from the definition of yeast, yeast would not be without sugar. Sugar is the *other-being* of yeast, as Hegel would say. Life is thus a relation, and if you - *in-vitro*-wise - cut off the organism from this relation, it becomes incomprehensible.

The principal definition of the phenomenon of life may therefore be expressed in subject-object terms in the following way. Life is a relation in which the one side actively (spending of energy) relates to the other side, which houses the first side's conditions of existence (as a source of potential energy).

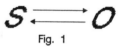

Fig. 1

The formulation of the general principle of life is not in itself a concrete scientific description of life's relation. For this purpose one requires the concrete physical, chemical, biochemical, cosmological, biogenetic and ecological studies that are presently beginning to open the door to the phenomenon of life.

Neither does the principle of life in itself say anything about the particular problem of behaviour, i.e. the principles that guide the monadic organism into opening and closing its window. Behaviour, of course, can only be understood against the background defined by the principles of life, but it cannot be identified with these principles. How the monad communicates with the world outside is a problem in its own right, and it is somewhere in this context that the phenomena of the psyche come into existence.

Stimulus-response

The fundamental concept in the study of behaviour has for several reasons been *stimulus-response* (S => R). Firstly, it springs from the philosophical paradigm of Galileian natural science emphasising cause and effect relationships of a mechanical nature. Secondly, it readily offers itself to experimental procedure, where effects are understood as the product of initial conditions under the control of the experimenter. Thirdly, it is a true reflection of a broad range of biological phenomena.

In our metaphor, stimulus-response means that first something taps on the window of the organism, after which the organism opens the window. The causal relation - initial event - secondary event - is very different, however, from ordinary mechanical causality. When you kick a ball the energy from the kick is transferred to the ball and makes it fly, but it is not the energy from the tap that opens the window. The stimulus and the response have no energetic correspondence. The organism itself opens the window, through energy of its own, and does so according to the information and not the energy of the stimulus.

The responsivity of the organism is thus a reflection of the general principle of life. In biology it is called *irritability* - defined by Leontiev "as the general property of all living bodies to enter into a state of activity through the effect of external influences" (Leontiev, 1981, p. 13).

The stimulus-response sequence involves two sets of control which should not be confused. The stimulus is in control because it causes the organism to act. The organism is in control because the response is its own doing. In the latter aspect the organism is fundamentally active. In the former it is passive, the initiative belonging to the stimulating agent. To express this double determination we will call the responding organism for *re-active*.

The prototype of this reactiveness is the sequence: (1) Contact with an object of food stimulates the organism (2) into an active response devouring the object of food, (3) which subsequently is consumed furnishing the organism with life-sustaining energy.

The middle term unavoidably introduces the concept of purpose, which is an anathema to the mechanical paradigm. The organism does something (2) to achieve something (3). That events or acts of behaviour are carried out with reference to some future situation is certainly the case here, thus the spectre of teleology arises.

The behavioural scientists have not evaded the issue, however. In nearly all texts on behaviour one finds arguments trying to circumvent the problem of teleology; and with no little success, as it proves.

Intention, function, and teleonomy

A noteworthy effort to refute teleological explanations is coinciding with the birth of a new science - cybernetics. Norbert Wiener's efforts during World War 2 to make British anti-aircraft guns goal-directed proved to his mind that goal-directedness fits fine with mechanics. Teleology is just negative feedback, he declared in 1943 together with Rosenblueth and Bigelow (Wiener, Rosenblueth & Bigelow, 1943). The same conclusion had been reached by W.R. Ashby: "The property of being 'goal-seeking' is not that of Life or Mind but of negative feedback (Ashby, 1948). Would anyone question his evidence, then a machine named 'Homeostat', designed to imitate certain features of behaviour, and Walter Grey's '"Machine Speculatrix" complete with motor, wheels, photo-electric receptors and 6-volt accumulator, would end all doubt.

The identification of life with negative feedback is erroneous, but the point about behaviour is not. The behaviour of the mechanical beetle, tortoise, or whatever is goal-directed, but it would be wrong to say that the robots have an intention. The purposiveness is a result of the design.

Here we can straight away see one of the argument's weaknesses. The mechanical animal had no intention, but its maker did. The issue of teleology is not refuted, only displaced.

This displacement is curiously reminiscent of predarwinian deism, which related the wonderfully adapted design of living nature to the providence of the Maker. The question to be answered, though, is how does one account for the seeming purposefulness of nature as a *natural* and not as an *artificial* phenomenon?

The efforts of cybernetics and deism have not been in vain, however. From the distinction between designer and design springs, the distinction between *intention* and *function*. The goal-seeking behaviour of the mechanical beetle is a function laid down in the design; the device has no intention. In the same way the gyration of the bean stalk is a function laid down in the design, and not an intention. The robot and the plant are goal-directed, but they are not in a true sense goal-intending. The goal-directed functionality of the artificial creature is easily accounted for - its designer intended it to behave in a purposeful way. But who designed the beautiful goal-directed functionality of the bean stalk? The answer, of course, is natural selection. There is no conscious aim of a designer in nature; the functional design of living organisms is the result of random variation and subsequent selection of the more functional designs, i.e. those with better life success. To explain the functionality of the bean stalk therefore requires the tracing of its concrete evolutionary history. What seems to be teleology is only adaptability, as Ashby says, and adaptability can be understood in terms of ordinary causality.

To distinguish the functional goal-directedness of all living organisms from the concept of genuine teleology, where a future situation is intended, Pittendrigh (1958) has suggested the term *teleonomy*, which can be defined as a planned activity that functions in a goal-directed way without knowledge of the goal. Teleonomy is thus "pseudo-purposeful functioning" (Luria, 1973, p. 80).

Three kinds of explanation

The concept of teleonomy expresses the complexity and historical nature of biological phenomena. In physical mechanics there is a direct and immediate connection between cause and effect, but the response of the living organism is not directly explainable from the stimulus that prompts it into action. H.S. Jennings formulates this in the following way in *Behaviour of the Lower Organisms*: "The reactions produced in unicellular organisms by stimuli are not the direct physical or chemical efforts of the agents acting upon them, but are indirect reactions, produced through the release of certain forces already present in the organisms" (Jennings, 1962, p. 261). The response therefore must be understood in terms of the design of the organism, and this again in terms of evolutionary history. Stimulus-response, seemingly a simple causal relationship, is thus a very complex one, which is only comprehensible from the perspective of relations beyond the immediate situation. Biology therefore has to distinguish between different levels of explanation.

Fraenkel and Gunn (1961, p. 16), in their classic study of animal orientation, specifically take this problem up in connection with the discussion of teleological explanations in biology.

They choose as an example the behaviour of woodlice. Woodlice aggregate in damp places, which is extremely appropriate considering that they desiccate in dry surroundings. The explanation that comes most immediately to mind is, therefore, that woodlice search for moist places with the intended aim of securing their lives.

However, this clearly teleological explanation gives the student of invertebrate behaviour plenty to think about. How do woodlice know the future situation? How can they aim for something not present?

They do not, as the scientific study of their behaviour proves. Through the mechanism of stimulus and response, the woodlice react to the immediate situation. They respond to the stimulus of dryness by speeding up their movement. The movement has no aim, it is not directed towards anything. Moving speedily in dry surroundings and slowly in moist nevertheless means that woodlice, all else being equal, spend more time in the preferable conditions. The aggregation thus follows from ecological laws of probability and does not even involve goal-directedness on the part of the animal.

This simple locomotive behaviour, *kinesis* in the language of invertebrate zoology, which actually orients the animal toward optimal conditions, but without any real orientation at all, is a perfect expression of the beauty of teleonomy.

Fraenkel and Gunn call the explanation expressed in terms of stimulus-response connections "the mechanical answer". We would call it the functional answer, and it still leaves unanswered how the function came about. This calls for "the evolutionary answer", as Fraenkel and Gunn rightly say, and they further point out that both the mechanical and the evolutionary answer are valid and belong together.

The teleological answer, however, is non-valid. At best it is an antropomorphism used for reasons of convenience and easy expression. The answer, that the organism does this with the aim of achieving that, should only be used as a sort of short-hand for the full evolutionary and functional explanation, which would be too cumbersome to repeat at every instance.

Evolutionary short-cuts

However, it is evident that human communication is not the only area in which it is expedient to short-cut the lengthy and complex workings of natural selection. It has happened in evolution itself. The adaptation of animal behaviour is not only determined by natural selection, i.e., on the level of species and of population genetics. It is also determined on the level of the individual. Learning, the individual ability to adapt behaviour to changing circumstances known in all animal forms, is a true short-cut of natural selection (favoured by natural selection, actually).

This does not mean that learning transgresses the bounds of teleonomy. The adaptability of the stimulus-response sequence known as classical and operant conditioning, for example, is in very nice agreement with the concept of teleonomy. But it means, that life is on the look out for advantageous short-cuts on the individual level. Behaviour guided by true intentionality would undoubtedly be such an advantageous short-cut, if developed.

Whether it has developed or not cannot be decided from philosophy, logic or the current concepts of natural science. It is solely an empirical question. As such it must be answered in the affirmative. Man has true intentionality, as described above by Brentano, Davydov and Zinchenko. True intentionality thus exists in the real world. This has been called psyche throughout the history of thought and its special quality is precisely the teleological, i.e. the genuine reference to a future situation or goal. The sole question, therefore, is how teleology came to exist in the teleonomic world of natural selection?

From irritability to sensibility

Lamarck recognized the importance of this question, for - as he writes in *Philosophie Zoologique* from 1809, "if nature were confined to the employment of its first means - namely, of a force entirely external and foreign to the animal - its works would have remained very incomplete; the animals would have remained machines totally passive" (cf Packard, 1901, p. 329)[12]. They are, however, not machines which is why a transformation must have occurred during the course of evolution from teleonomical irritability to a proper form of subjectivity. We can imagine, writes Lamarck, "how the force which excites the organic movements may, in the simplest animals, be outside of them and yet animate them; how, then, this force has been transported and fixed in the animal itself; finally, how it then has become the source of sensibility, and in the end of acts of intelligence" (ibid., p. 281). The subjective sensibility which

---

[12]   Corrected from the original by the author.

develops from simple irritability "constitutes this me (moi) with which all ani-mals, which are only sensitive, are penetrated, without perceiving it, but which those possessing a brain are able to notice..." (ibid., p. 325). But Lamarck con-cedes that this "feeling of existence (sentiment d'existence), which I shall call *inner feeling*, ... is a very obscure feeling" (ibid.).

A very obscure concept also, we should add. Lamarck has not solved the problem, only identified it. The identification, however, is a magnificent achievement. The key to understanding the psyche is the transformation of irritability into sensibility.

This is also precisely how A.N. Leontiev understands it. In his doctoral dissertation from 1940 on *The problem of the origin of sensation*, he writes that "from the angle of our hypothesis, sensitivity arises as a rudimentary form of psychic reflection, during the evolution of simple irritability that is inherent in any viable body, even the simplest" (Leontiev, 1981, p. 51). Then he imme-diately makes it clear "that our hypothesis rejects from the start any attempt to approach reflection from the angle of the notorious 'principle of the specific energy of the sense organs' (J. Müller)" (ibid.). In other words, the explana-tion of how this primitive psyche comes into being must live in accordance with the pact of four. This does not mean, however, that the specific quality of psyche can be reduced away. "Mind is a property of living, highly organised material bodies that consists in their ability to reflect in subjective experienc-ing the reality around them, which exists independently of them" (ibid., p. 18).[13]

Subjective experiencing amounts to no more than Lamarck's inner feel-ing, it is merely an identification of the phenomenon to be explained. This is important enough, but the interesting thing is, how Leontiev conceives the transformation of irritability into sensibility and how this relates to his general theory of activity.

Theory of activity

The theory of activity is an unique attempt to overcome the chasm between the classical materialistic stance emphasising one-sidedly the objective determination, hence the cognitive content or the known (O = > S), and the classical idealistic stance emphasising one-sidedly the subjective determinat-ion, hence the conative or the act of the knower (S = > O). It is thus an at-tempt to apply within the field of general psychology the insights of dialectical materialism, which was born from the problem of the subjective and the ob-jective.

---

13   Corrected from the German translation.

In the very first of the *Theses on Feuerbach*, with which Karl Marx in 1845 embarks upon his monumental scientific-philosophical undertaking, he writes: "The chief defect of all previous materialism is that things, reality, sensuousness are conceived only in the form of the *object, or of contemplation*, but not as *sensuous human activity, practice*, not subjectively. Hence, in contradistinction to materialism, the *active* side, was set forth abstractly by idealism, - which, of course, does not know real, sensuous activity as such" (Marx & Engels, 1976, p. 615). Therefore the necessity of a new concept of materialism able to encompass the facts of real subjective activity in a real objective world.

This insight was not wasted on the young Soviet psychology, led by inspired Vygotsky it set out to remedy the inability of Feuerbach to "conceive human activity itself as *objective* activity" (ibid.).

Naturally, man was the first priority of the Cultural-historical School of Vygotsky and his team. In particular, ontogenetic studies demonstrating how the mind is objectively formed (O = > S) through the child's active appropriation (S = >O) of the language and implements of the culture into which it is born. At some point, however, it became evident that the concept of object-determined activity should be enlarged to cover the development of mind in general. This task befell Leontiev, who set out to find the foundations of the psyche in biological evolution. The result of this quest is the general theory of activity, which has had a great impact on contemporary psychological thinking.[14]

If the aim of the Cultural-historical School's programme was to make room for the active subject (S = > O) in the objective psychology (O = > S) of Sechenov's Russian followers and of the American behaviourists, it did this very literally. In between the O and the S was placed the S = > O. Leontiev writes: "Thus, in psychology the following alternative was devised: either to keep the basic two-stage formula: action of the object = > change in ongoing condition of the subject (or which is essentially the same thing, the formula S = > R) or to devise a three-stage formula including a middle link ("middle term") - the activity of the subject and, correspondingly, conditions, goals and means of that activity - a link that mediates the ties between them" (Leontiev, 1978, p. 50).

The ensuing sequence could be written 1) O = > S, 2) S = > O, 3) O = > S, where the difference between 1 and 3 is that the latter O is determined through the activity of the subject. Reflection is thus the simultaneous result of objective reality and subjective activity directed towards this reality; the knower and the known has equal importance.

---

[14] See f.example the Proceedings of the 1st International Congress on Activity Theory vol.1-4, Berlin 1986.

The bifurcation

The transformation of irritability (simple stimulus-response) into sensibility and thus the genesis of psyche should, according to Leontiev, be understood as the conversion of O => S into the tripartite sequence early in animal evolution. Leontiev does not exclude an "elementary sensory psyche" in higher infusoria.

The decisive point of the conversion is the transition from 1 to 2 in the sequence. The animal begins to relate differently to the properties of the object. That, which in irritability was merely a stimulus, has become a signal, one might say.

The peculiarity of sensibility, - "which, although a certain form of irritability, is, however, a qualitative unique form" (Leontiev, 1981, p. 13) - is ascribed by Leontiev to a fundamental bifurcation in the evolution of living matter: "Some of the environment's influences affected the organism as determinants (positive or negative) of its very existence, others only as stimuli and directors of its activity." This split was accompanied by a corresponding differentiation of the functions of the organism. "On the one hand processes that were directly linked with the support and maintenance of life became differentiated... On the other hand processes became differentiated that did not directly have life-supporting functions and simply mediated an organism's links with those properties of the environment on which its existence depended. They constituted a special form of vital activity that also underlay organisms' sensitivity and their psychic reflection of the properties of the external environment" (ibid., p. 45).

This important distinction could be exemplified by the nutritious property of the food-particle and the mechanical property of the same food-particle that induces the worm to engulf it. The first property is life-sustaining, the latter signaling or activity-mediating.

Or, it could be exemplified by the sound of the keeper's steps, which signal the meat-powder, in anticipation of which the dog begins to salivate. Leontiev sets the stage for this interpretation when he writes: "Pavlov assumes the difference between unconditioned and conditioned reflexes, and connects them with the fundamental biological difference between the two forms of connection the organism has with its surroundings - the direct connection and the signalling connection. This differentiation is very significant for the general theory of sensation. Through it the understanding of sensation's signalling, orienting function could be introduced in psychology" (Leontiev, 1977, p. 227-228).

A Pavlovian psyche?

Does Leontiev conceive the origin of psyche as the result of a process similar to the stimulus-response transformation of classical conditioning? It seems so. But Leontiev is ambiguous, and this conception, which turns activity into an intervening variable in what is basically a stimulus-response sequence, is in poor agreement with the essence of his general theory. Leontiev says himself about the S = > R scheme, that "no complication of the original scheme .... is capable of abolishing the methodological difficulties which this scheme has presented to psychology" (Leontiev, 1978, p. 49). But his theory, formulated as a three-stage scheme, actually appears as precisely such a complication of the original scheme. Davydov raises the same problem: "In our opinion, the concepts of stimulus and response in the first schema preclude any objective determination and associated activation in the form of exploratory movements... Therefore, the concept of activity should not make the two-term schema more precise, but rather eliminate it" (Davydov, 1981, p. 17).

In my view Leontiev has uncovered a decisive truth in his theory of activity, which he misses in his account of the origin of the psyche.[15] Remember that the first psyche is also the general psyche, and thus the essence of our mind. If psyche can be reduced to the stimulus-substitution of classical conditioning, this is the essence of every psyche from the lowest to the highest.

The theory of activity, of course, contradicts such a deficient view of psychic life, which throws the understanding back to the misguided efforts of the behaviourists. This inconsistency in the thinking of Leontiev, however, is ideally suited for our purpose, as it demonstrates the very problem which must be overcome if the foundation of psyche is to be understood. Namely, the problem of making a real separation of the teleological sensibility from the teleonomic irritability.

You will have noticed, for example, that the tripartite sequence of Leontiev is very akin to our tripartite prototype of reactivity described earlier. The latter could also be written 1) O = > S, 2) S = > O, 3) O = > S. Equally, it is difficult to see that Leontiev's distinction between the life-sustaining influence and the signaling stimulus (mental reflection) is not the same as our distinction between the food-property and the window-tapping property of the organism's object. But this distinction in the relation between subject and object is carried by any form of life, goes with the definition of stimulus-response, and hence with the definition of life itself. Like his great

---

[15] It should be mentioned that Leontiev - together with Zaporoshets - foistered the Pavlovian idea of psyche in 1936, in which year a Stalinist purge banned the Cultural-historical School and ordered psychology to follow in the footsteps of physiology.

predecessors, Lamarck as well as Aristotle, Leontiev here fails to make a true distinction between the phenomenon of life and the phenomenon of psyche.

The qualification made between the unconditioned and the conditioned stimulus does not turn the trick. Psyche cannot be reduced to the way the window is tapped; it cannot be encompassed within the bounds of the $S => R$ scheme. (If it could, the cyberneticists would carry the day). What we should be looking for is a completely new quality making a vast difference, not just complex variants of stimulus-response. This defines the task before us. We will now search for a different way in which irritability could have been transformed into sensibility in the early evolution of animal life.

The world of simple behaviour

By choosing the Pavlovian model or metaphor, Leontiev emphasises psyche as the objective content of reflection ($O => S$). This classical *cognitive* definition of psyche, has an alternative, as Aristotle wrote. Namely, "the view that the soul is a self-moving entity". We will take this *conative* understanding as our starting point. By emphasising psyche as a subjective act of reflection ($S => O$), we do not fail to appreciate the aspect of objective cognition. But this in itself does not constitute psyche.

Emphasising the acts of the subject, we should begin our quest at the level of simple teleonomic behaviour. We have already described the two principal types of behaviour at this level. The first is our prototype of reactivity, in which contact with a positive stimulus (food) prompts the organism into making a consummatory response. The second - exemplified by Fraenkel and Gunn's woodlice - is that in which a negative stimulus causes the organism to respond with kinesis. The latter is locomotion, the animal (plants have no locomotion) moves from one place to another, which is more optimal. Though kinesis is goal-directed in the sense that the movement indirectly relates to a future situation, it is completely controlled by the stimulus of the immediate situation. As a functional response kinesis is simply negative feedback. The connection between the response and the happy outcome is purely the result of the ingenuity of natural selection. The consummatory response and the kinesis are opposite responses in as much as the first is grabbing for the good things in life, while the latter is trying to escape the bad, but they are identical in the sense that they share the essence of reactivity, teleonomic functionality and irritability. Thus, they are definitely non-psychic.

The situations in which the monad reacts adequately when fortune or misfortune knocks on its window, do not, however, exhaust the possible vital situations that the monad might encounter. There is also the situation when nothing knocks. We should consider not only the positivity and negativity of the stimuli, but also the presence and absence of the stimuli. This gives us the four different prototypical situations seen in fig. 2, which should be distinguished from each other.

Situations 1 and 2 are already accounted for. The first is kinesis, where the stimulus is present and negative, the second is the consummatory response, where the stimulus is present and positive. Situation 3 hardly needs any consideration. The absence of negative stimuli constitutes no problem for the animal, on the contrary, it is the criterion for the success of kinesis. This leaves us with situation 4.

	Present	Nonpresent
Negative	1	3
Positive	2	4

Fig. 2

A vital problem

Situation 4 constitutes a problem, which might even be critical for the animal. The absence of the positive stimulus and thereby the trigger for the consummatory response simply means a barred access to food, which if continued would eventually lead to the death of the animal.

The solution to this problem would be locomotion, of course, in order to reach out into time and space searching for the stimulus. Kinesis made it possible for the woodlice to move from threatening surroundings into more beneficial, could not the same mechanism direct the simple animal from surroundings devoid of food into more promising ones?

No, it could not. Absence of the positive stimulus is no less a misfortune than the presence of the negative stimulus, but there is a world of difference, which renders the mechanism of kinesis useless in the first case. Kinesis is a response controlled by an external stimulus, if there is no external stimulus, there can be no kinesis. To allow the absence of a stimulus to be a stimulus, perhaps named need[16], would be to confound the whole issue. The problem of situation 4 cannot be solved within the stimulus-response scheme.

Auto-kinesis

Let us approach the problem from the engineering angle of Ashby and Walter Grey and ask, how the kinesis should be reconstructed to handle the absence of the positive stimulus? The answer is simple, the switch should be reversed!

---

[16] Need as a psychological category is not hereby refuted. Need, however, is not a basic but a higher-order category. The understanding of psyche cannot be based on the concept of need, on the contrary, the concept of need must be based on an understanding of the relations of psyche.

While in Fraenkel and Gunn's kinesis there is straightforward proportionality between stimulation and movement, here there needs to be reversed proportionality. When there is no positive stimulus the 'speeder' should be on and be shut off at contact with the stimulus, whereupon the consummatory response takes over. Whenever in a field without food the animal would be on the move, and according to the same ecological probabilities that brought the woodlice from dry to moist surroundings, the subject would eventually happen upon its life-sustaining object.

This would mean, however, that the animal would be in locomotion whenever it is not provoked to a halt by some external or internal influence. Active movement would then be the normal state of such an animal.

The demands on energy, of course, would be enormous. But this in itself does not disqualify this design. It greatly enhances the chance of getting to the object, and if this advantage exceeds the cost of unceasing movement, it could be favoured by natural selection. Apparently it was.

We could call moving activity unprovoked by any stimulus or outer influence self-movement or *auto-kinesis*, the very word Aristotle uses.[17] The parallel latin word for that which happens of its own accord, without external influence, is spontane, and spontaneous activity is a reality of life, as the students of invertebrate behaviour learned, some to their dismay.

Spontaneity of behaviour

The import of the new hard-science physiology reached behavioural zoology at the same time it reached psychology. Jacques Loeb from the University of Würzburg became "the prophet of the new movement", as Fraenkel and Gunn write. "Starting in 1888, he set his face against anthropomorphism and teleology in the study of invertebrate behaviour and began the attempt to describe all behaviour in physical and chemical terms" (Fraenkel & Gunn, 1961, p. 6). It was his general idea that animal locomotion could be explained in the same terms as the movements of plants, i.e. as direct effects of a field of forces. Duly enlarged "the tropism theory might include human conduct also", Loeb (1919, p. 171) writes.

Incidentally, as proof of his "Mechanistic Conception of Life" (the title of his book from 1912) he points to the "artificial heliotropic machine" constructed by Hammond according to Loeb's ideas!

But, alas, life is no machine. Already in 1889 Verworn convincingly established that spontaneous behaviour, irreconcilable with Loeb's scheme, was a fact of invertebrate life. In his famous work *Behaviour of the Lower Organisms* from 1906 the great authority in this field, Herbert Spencer Jennings, con-

---

17   Aristotle: De Anima, 406b 5-10.

cludes: "A first and essential point for the understanding of behaviour is that activity occurs in organisms without present external stimulation. The normal condition of the Paramecium is an active one, with its cilia in rapid movement; it is only under special conditions that it can be brought partly to rest... The organism *is* activity, and its activities may be spontaneous, so far as the present external stimuli are concerned" (Jennings, 1962, p. 284).

The spontaneity of behaviour is in no way mystical. It does not contradict the pact of the four. "The movements are undoubtedly the expression of energy derived from metabolism", Jennings writes. "The organism continually takes in energy with its food... and continually gives off this energy in activities of various sorts. The point of importance is that this activity often depends more largely on the past external conditions through which the energy was stored up than upon present ones" (ibid.). The behaviour, thus, is not un-caused. It is founded on the laws of biochemistry and metabolism as expressed through the particular structure and history of the animal. In relation to the surrounding environment, however, it is un-caused; no external stimuli prod it along. This is what spontaneity of behaviour means.

Reversal

Being a result of structure and history, autokinesis no less than ordinary kinesis is a teleonomic phenomenon. Just as the kinetic escape from threatening surroundings is biologically meaningful, so too is the kinetic search for promising ones. Both functions share the purpose of securing and sustaining life, but the purposiveness of the designs lies with natural selection and nowhere else.

Their common teleonomic foundation acknowledged, ordinary kinesis and autokinesis nevertheless are very different. The former aims for an undisturbed state. It is thus in harmony with Walter B. Cannon's concept of homeostasis, where the responses through the means of negative feedback serve to restore the tranquil state, the optimum. It could thus be termed *servo-kinesis* in reference to the servo-mechanistic function. The latter, on the other hand, aims for the very opposite: stimulus, disturbance, input, food. It is an appetitive function and reflects the fundamental greedy nature of life, which is better portrayed by the workings of positive feed-back.

However, that which first and foremost interests us is the decisively different way in which the two types of kinesis relate to the surrounding environment, i.e. to the biologically meaningful stimulus relevant in each case.

Servo-kinesis is a model example of the stimulus-response scheme and represents a direct relationship with controlling environmental variables.

Auto-kinesis, on the other hand, per definition defies the stimulus-response sequence, since the response appears spontaneously or prior to the biologically meaningful stimulus. There is no direct relationship between the behaviour of the subject and the sought for stimulus. No chain of physical-chemical events causally connects the two. The moving animal receives no controlling influence in the form of energy or information from its teleonomic target.

This does not mean, however, that auto-kinesis fails to establish a relation to the food-object. The whole teleonomic meaning of the auto-kinesis is the establishment of precisely such a relationship. Only it is a relationship of a different order.

In order to understand the difference between the environmental relations set up by servo-kinesis and auto-kinesis respectively, we should distinguish three different levels of relation: the vital or biological, the environmental and the behavioural. The first is the vital meaning (negative or positive) of some factor or object to the life-success of the animal. The second is the response-demanding distribution (presence or absence) of this factor in the animal's life-world. The third is the way the animal responds and moves in relation to this factor and its temporal-spatial distribution.

In servo-kinesis the three levels are virtually collapsed into one. The non-directed escape movement is triggered (3) by the immediate contact (2) with an environmental factor which is very detrimental to the animal's health (1), e.g. dryness in the case of woodlice. It is one inseparable event carried by the stimulus-response sequence.

In auto-kinesis, on the other hand, the levels are truly separated. The relation between subject and object, the organism and its food, is vital (1) to the degree that it determines and defines life. Environmentally, however, the subject and object are disconnected due to the absence of food in the animal's immediate surroundings (2). Therefore, the auto-kinetic behaviour is set up (teleonomically) to realise the environmentally unrealised vital relation (3).

The project of servo-kinesis is to disconnect the environmentally connected. Servo-kinesis therefore proceeds from the connection, as happens in the stimulus-response sequence. The project of auto-kinesis is to connect the environmentally disconnected. Here there is no connection to proceed from, therefore the teleonomic necessity of spontaneous locomotion, or the reversal of the stimulus-response sequence. In servo-kinesis the relationship to the vital factor in the external environment is reactive. In auto-kinesis it has to be active.

The alternative

As ascertained by Jennings, auto-kinesis based on spontaneity is no less a fact of life than servo-kinesis based on stimulus-response. Here, then, we have the alternative to the $S => R$ model, which Davydov found irreconcilable with the theory of activity. The concept of activity developed by Leontiev is much more compatible with the subjective self-activity of auto-kinesis. Actually, what he pursues in his works on activity from infusoria to man is essentially this.

The auto-kinesis is simply the first form of activity, understood as a behaviour relating, not just responding, to the external world. Hence auto-kinesis offers an alternative opening to the understanding of psyche, which does not get bogged down by the trappings of stimulus-response and conditioning.

What kept Leontiev from this conclusion which is so much demanded by his own works? A very good reason, I presume. The essential aspect of psyche in Leontiev's understanding is the cognitive. The reflection of the objective world ($O = >S$). Auto-kinesis, devoid of any stimulus input, offers no such thing. It seems to be pure subjective conation ($S = >$); the latter term denoting nothing more than the spontaneous movement of the organism as described above, and thus fully agreeing with the pact of four.

This brings us back to the discussion between Henrik Poulsen and myself. Neither Leontiev nor Henrik Poulsen were wrong in emphasising the cognitive aspect as the *sine qua non* of psyche. But is auto-kinesis really devoid of this decisive aspect? With this question we are approaching the crux of the whole matter.

The riddle of the absent present

The contradiction mentioned by Davydov and Zinchenko appears in auto-kinesis as well. The effort to connect the disconnected presupposes in itself the connection. It simply implies that the unrealised link between subject and object, that the auto-kinesis tries to realise, is already a reality. The absent must already be present!

This riddle is easily solved, however, when we make use of our distinctions. Biologically the subject and the object, the organism and its food, are inseparably connected. Not only does this relation define life, it also determines life. The object is the other-being of the subject. As long as the organism is living, and thus a subject, its biological relation to the food is always a very present reality.

Environmentally, however, the subject can be, and often is, separated from its food. This absence of the food-object (and hereby the absence of the positive stimulus for the consummatory response) also confronts the organism as a reality.

The behaviour of auto-kinesis as designed by natural selection serves to bridge the two realities, so the environmental reality does not refute the biological. Auto-kinesis is at the same time a behavioural expression of the connection and of the disconnection between subject and object.

Being a reflection of the absent object, and thus of the object, auto-kinesis is definitely cognitive behaviour. Cognition refers to objective relations of the external world as they are reflected by the subject, and the external world's objective relations are certainly being reflected in auto-kinesis, since the presence or absence of the object is an even more basic objective relation than the magnitude, distance and direction of the object. The most basic of all, actually.

The particular reflection of the object in auto-kinesis is, however, prior to the stimulus, and is thus more in accordance with the understanding of the rationalists than with the understanding of the empiriscists. This reminds us of the famous exchange between Locke and Leibniz, the latter answering the Englishman's claim, "that there is nothing in the mind, which was not first in the senses", with the retort: "Nothing except the mind itself!" The mind is not a board upon which the world writes (O = >S), it is subjective, cognising activity (S = >O). Exactly the point later made by Brentano.

Psyche

Without any infraction of the physiologists' pact, auto-kinesis could be called exactly subjective, cognising activity. Does that mean that we attribute the quality of psyche to auto-kinesis?

Yes, it does. The immanent objectivity or intentional inexistence, which we in accordance with Brentano have defined as the hall-mark of the psychic, is exactly the relation auto-kinesis establishes to its object. The locomotion is a biological expression of the object, which is not present, but searched for. It thus belongs to "such phenomena as include an object intentionally within themselves", which is Brentano's definition of psychic phenomena.

The immanent objectivity or intentional inexistence of the object is beautifully expressed by the reversal of the stimulus-response sequence in auto-kinesis. The reversed sequence would be response-stimulus. This is apparently a contradictio in adjecto, since the effect appears prior to the cause. But it is not biologically meaningless. Teleonomically spontaneous locomotion is a response to the object, which is nonpresent. Hence the immanent objectivity of auto-kinesis. In this way the object is the cause of the locomotion, only it is a cause that lies in the future not in the past. Such a cause is a goal. By the same reversal the future stimulus directing the responce is a motive. The object is materially non-present, but in the movement of the animal it is present as intention and goal. Auto-kinesis represents the first case of "the fundamental, cardinal aspect of the vital activity of every sentient being - a subject". In the words of Davydov and Zinchenko: "To look for something that does not yet exist but that is possible and is presented to the subject only as a goal, something that exists as an idea and is not yet actual".

41

The term idea expresses the same as Brentano's immanent objectivity. From the double existence of the object as being in the world and as being in the reflection of the subject rises the concepts of the material being and the ideal being. Both beings are real. Auto-kinesis is an ideal expression of the material object. This ideal expression is also the cognitive aspect of psyche. Likewise it is the intentional aspect. In auto-kinesis the conative act and the cognitive content are indivisible. This oneness of act and content, however, is another important characteristic of psyche. Objective reflection is not the unshared property of the psyche. It is a property of all matter.[18] It is the *subjective reflecting* of the objective that sets psyche apart. This is what Leontiev has in mind when he defines psyche as the living organisms' "ability to reflect in *subjective experiencing* the reality around them (italics added)".

The final mark of psyche is not wanting either. If auto-kinesis is a reversal of the causal relationship of the stimulus-response sequence, whereafter the animal moves with reference to a future goal rather than according to past or present influence, then it, of course, represents a true teleological relationship. The animal is not stirred into action by some stimulus, prior to any stimulus it is actively reaching out in time and space for its object.

The reversal represents the real difference between irritability and sensibility. In relation to the external world the organism in the first case (S => R) is little more than the object of the stimulus hitting it. In the last case (R => S) the animal is a true subject, de facto moving out to meet the stimulus. Put in terms of subject and object, the (O => S) of the first case is in the last case preceded by the (S => O). On one side we have just (O => S), on the other we have (S => O => S), which of course recalls the exchange between Locke and Leibniz, the latter denying that mind is a sitting duck.

The difference is very great between a stimulus 'received' and a stimulus 'perceived', that is read into the activity or performance of the subject. It is the experimental well known difference between simple afference and reafference. Actually, Leontiev was confronted with precisely this difference in his experiments on the genesis of feelings, which forced him to conclude that "a necessary condition for the rise of the studied sensations is a presence of a certain directed activity of the subject" (Leontiev, 1981, p. 68). "This meant *that the process resulting in the emergence of sensitivity to an ordinary unsensed agent and the forming of a conditioned-reflex association were not identical processes*" (ibid., p. 108). We would have added the italics, had Leontiev not done so himself.

---

[18]   See Jens Mammen's paper in this volume for a dialectical-materialistic analysis of the general reflecting essence of all matter, that is the extraction or abstraction of objective properties through relations.

The (S = > O = > S) chain defining the psychic could also be written in this way (S = >O)(O = >S). It has exactly the same structure as the schemata defining life (fig. 1). Psyche thus is a generalisation or extension of the principle of life. The biological principle is extended to a behavioural-environmental principle. From the biological subjectness of the monad develops the psychological subjectness of the active organism relating to the world. Irritability is transformed into sensibility.

Two realities linked

Auto-kinesis represents a real somersault in the development of life, but this does not mean that auto-kinesis is not still just auto-kinesis. The concepts of subjective activity, cognising act, immanent objectivity, intentional inexistence, motive, goal and idea, notwithstanding, auto-kinesis is perfectly - and only - explainable in the earlier mentioned physical-chemical and biological concepts of negative entropy, metabolism, function and teleonomy. Very likely spontaneous locomotion is the freak result of the accidental incorporation of microtubuli into some primordial cells; microtubuli being complex molecular structures with the odd physical-chemical property of perpetual movement, thus furnishing the monads with an organ and source of spontaneous locomotion. This fortuitous development would be in complete harmony with the pact of the four, entirely within the understanding of modern physics, biochemistry and biology. Nothing but chance, natural law and natural selection would be called for to explain it, the evident purposiveness of the thing being only a case of teleonomic functionality.

What it does mean, however, is that with the arrival of the purely biophysical phenomenon of auto-kinesis an entirely new relation is brought into existence. Namely, the teleological relation between the subject and the object, meaning that the subject de facto acts with reference to a future goal. This subjective relating is *psyche* and its qualities are intention, goal, idea, motive, etc, which qualities are brought into existence by the sheer fact of autokinetic locomotion. Psyche, thus, is not a substance or a force. It is an expression of a unique material relationship in the world, as are all the basic steps on the cosmogenetic ladder, the nuclear, the atomic, the chemical, the living.

Each step on the ladder is connected to the prior, and yet altogether its own, as is always the case with development. On the foundations of physics, chemistry and biology thus is born an entirely new reality with its own unique principles or logic, therefore requiring its own science and its own concepts. The new science is psychology.

Auto-kinesis thus links two separate scientific realities, like the electron shell of the atom links the separate scientific realities of atomic physics and chemistry. Such material linkage is always the case between neighbouring sciences on the evolutionary scale. This is what we meant, when we said that the origin of the psyche is beyond psychology. The science of psychology must begin with the psyche as a positive fact.

Definition

The short, positive definition of psyche is teleological activity. It is from this fact that thinkers have proceeded throughout history. It is nevertheless very important to include in the definition the complex material evolution that brought the psyche into existence and thus the complex interconnections between the sciences. Summing up the above would be an attempt at such a definition.

1. Given life, that is the biological relation between subject and object, and thus, given the vital necessity of the object as other-being for the subject (all founded on bio-physical relations as developed during early chemical evolution);
2. Given an environmental field in which there are no objects of food in the immediate surroundings of the animal, but where objects of food are obtainable at some distance;
3. Given the spontaneous locomotion of the animal (which itself is founded on bio-physical relations as developed during the natural selection of early organisms);
4. Given these, the locomotion will by the laws of probability eventually result in contact between the subject and its object, even though no stimulus is guiding the locomotion.
5. This means that the locomotive behaviour establishes a *real* connection to *the absent object*, despite the fact that there is no immediate material contact in the form of energy or information between the subject and the object.
6. The reality of this non-material connection as expressed through the activity of the subject we term *psyche*. As a reflection of the non-present object we term the processes associated with the movement the *ideal* expression of the object. It is synonymous with the term *immanent objectivity*. The concepts of ideality and immanent objectivity are necessary to express the fact that there is a real relation (real in terms of life and death) between subject and object, which is not carried by any material input from the outside. As the vital necessity of reaching the object is the biological basis of the spontaneous locomotion, we express this by talking about the *intentional inexistence of the object* in the activity of the subject. This is synonymous with the term *goal*. Being goal-intended activity we also use the term *teleological* for the active relation between the subject and the object.
7. The teleological activity belongs to the class of teleonomic relations, its purposiveness being a result of natural selection. It differs from non-

teleological relations, however, in the way the purposiveness is mediated. In non-teleological reactivity the purposiveness is mediated through causal chains of external influence. Lacking this material basis the organism must itself (through spontaneous locomotion) mediate the life-sustaining relation to its object. This is what teleological means.

This definition, by the way, also tells us when the relation of psyche first came into existence. It came into existence with the first case of spontaneous loco-motion, which effectively changed the probability of reaching non-present food. No doubt, this was early in evolution. Personally I fancy the protozoans as the first organisms partaking in this new reality, rapidly moving their cilia or whipping their tails, but most likely it was already some bacteria, hard as it may be to connect bacteria with anything psychic. The simplicity of the or-ganism, however, has nothing to do with it. Psyche is not an inner property of the organism requiring some special structure or equipment. It is a particular relation in the world brought about solely as the consequence of spontaneous locomotion as spelled out in the definition. This is why sessile forms of life, like plants, do not have psyche.

The reality of psyche

Does this make our definition of psyche an operational definition? Yes, it cer-tainly has much in common with H.S. Jennings' famous anchoring of psychic terms to objective criteria of behaviour in chapter 20 of *Behaviour of the Lower Organisms*. When the animal moves in this particular manner in relation to its object, this is psyche, we say, implying nothing else than the observable feat-ures of the behaviour and the way it relates to the environment.

This does not mean, however, that it is a descriptive or nominal definit-ion referring only to the use people make of words. The behaviourists-to-be understood Jennings in this way, when he compared the reactions of amoeba with the psychic manifestations of man and wrote: "Thus it seems possible to trace back to the lowest organisms some of the phenomena which we know, from objective evidence, to exist in the behaviour of man and the higher ani-mals, and which have received special names" (Jennings, 1962, p. 355). To Watson and his comrades-in-arms psychic references were only special names, and so a whole new branch of science was founded on the misconception that psyche is a product of language and an epiphenomenon.

Our operational definition is a *real* definition referring to objective properties of the world. When we define psyche as a certain set of biological, environmental and behavioural relations, this does not make psyche an epiphenomenon. Psyche is no more an epiphenomenon than elephants or traffic jams. Psyche is a real relation coming into existence in the real world. Jennings knew this too. Sharing "the ideal of most scientific men", namely "to explain behaviour in terms of matter and energy, so that the introduction of psychic implications is considered superfluous" (ibid., p. 329), he nevertheless had to admit the real subjectivity of the organism: "In conducting objective investigations we train ourselves to suppress this impression, but thorough investigation tends to restore it stronger than at first" (ibid., p. 336).

The final touchstone of biological reality is natural selection, and natural selection has not failed to prove the reality of psyche. Being a real relation determining the life success of the animal, psyche was soon worked upon by the forces of evolution. Any variation improving the teleological short-cut of teleonomical purposiveness was favoured. From the blind auto-kinesis of the monad evolved forms of cognising locomotion that could reach further and further out in time and space. New organs of locomotion evolved hand in hand with new organs of sensation. Brains evolved to accommodate the computation of the yet unseen. At some point, what we call mind evolved, the ability to monitor not only the world but the relation to the world as well. Finally, the consciousness of the human being evolved.

These steps in the ladder of psychogenesis should not be confused, each has added a new quality to the reality of psyche. All the evolutionary forms of psyche share, however, the fundamental essence of psyche.

"Action is as spontaneous in the protozoa as in man", Jennings writes (ibid., p. 261), and from this spontaneity or freedom of external control rises the teleological relation of psyche, when the *free* subject moves to realise the *necessity* of the object. From monad to man psyche is self-movement and cognition united in the self-willed goal-intending act. Or put in the words of Wilhelm Wundt from *Grundzüge der physiologischen Psychologie*: "What confronts us as the typical forms of psycho-physical events from the simplest spontaneous movements of the protozoans to man's highest manifestations of life, is voluntary activity" (Wundt, 1903, p. 744).

References

Ashby, W.R. (1948), Design for a brain, *Electronic Engineering*, vol. 20.

Baumer, Le van (1978), *Main currents of western thought*, New Haven & London.

Boring, E. (1950), *A history of experimental psychology*, 2. edition, New York.

Braun, K.H., W.Hollitscher, K. Holzkamp & K. Wetzel (1983), *Karl Marx und die Wissenschaft vom Individuum* (Karl Marx and the science of the individual), Marburg.

Brentano, F. (1874), *Psychologie vom empirischen Standpunkte* (Psychology from an empirical point of view), Leipzig. Transl. John J. Sullivan: 'Franz Brentano and the problems of intentionality' in B.B. Wolman (ed.): Historical roots of contemporary psychology, New York and London, 1968, p. 248-274.

Darwin, C. (1889), *The descent of man and selection in relation to sex*, 2. edition, London.

Davydov, V.V. & V.P. Zinchenko (1981), The principle of development in psychology, *Soviet Psychology*, 20, no. 1.

Davydov, V.V. (1981), 'Activity and reflection in Leontiev's theory', *Soviet Psychology*, 19, no. 4.

Dyson, F. (1985), *Origins of life*, Cambridge.

Engelsted, N. (1981), *Om den politiske natur* (On the political nature), Copenhagen.

Fraenkel, G.S. & D.L. Gunn (1961), *The orientation of animals*, New York.

Hammond, W.A. (1902), *Aristotle's Psychology*, New York.

Jennings, H.S. (1962), *Behavior of the lower organisms* (org. 1906), Indiana.

Lamarck, J.B. (1802), *Recherches sur l'organisation der corps vivans* (Research on the organisation of the living body), cf. A.S. Packard: Lamarck, The founder of evolution, New York, London & Bombay 1901, p.158.

Lamarck, J.B. (1815-22), *Histoire naturelle*. Cf. John Greene: The death of Adam, Iowa 1959, p. 155.

Lamarck, J.B. (1830), *Philosophie Zoologique*, 2. edition, Paris.

LaMettrie, J.O. (1748), *L'Homme machine*. Cf. R.J. Herrnstein & G. Boring: A sourcebook in the history of psychology, Mass. 1965.

Leontiev, A.N. (1977), 'Om den sanselige genspejlings mekanisme' (On the sensual mechanism of reflection), in *Problems of the development of mind*, Danish edition, Copenhagen.

Leontiev, A.N. (1978), *Activity, consciousness and personality*, Englewood Cliffs, N.J.

Leontiev, A.N. (1981), *Problems of the development of mind*, Moscow.

Loeb, J. (1919), *Forced movements, tropisms and animal conduct*, Philadelphia and London.

Luria, S.E. (1973), *Life, the unfinished experiment*, New York.

Marx, K. & F.Engels (1976), *The german ideology*, Moscow.

Packard, A.S. (1901), *Lamarck, The founder of evolution. His life and works. With translation of his writing on organic evolution*, New York, London and Bombay.

Pittendrigh, C.(1958), 'Natural selection and behavior', in A. Roe & G.G. Simpson (eds.): Behavior and Evolution, New Haven, p. 390-416.

Poulsen, H. (1982), Leontjew, genspejlingsbegrebet og den almene psykologi (Leontiev, the concept of reflectivity and general psychology), *Psyke & Logos*, *1*, p. 161-175.

Poulsen, H. (1986), Konationer (Conations), *Psyke og Logos*, 2, p. 289-317.

Ray, J. (1701): *The Wisdom of God Manifested in the Works of the Creation*, 3. edition, London.

Schrödinger, E. (1944), *What is life? The physical aspect of the living cell,* Cambridge.

Spencer, H. (1855), *Principles of psychology,* London.

Wiener, N., A.Rosenblueth & J.Bigelow (1943), Behavior, purpose and teleology, *Philosophy of Science,* vol.10.

Wundt, W. (1903), *Grundzüge der physiologischen Psychologie,* 5. edition, Leipzig.

The Phylogenesis and Sociogenesis of the Psyche and the Law of Correspondence

Boje Katzenelson

The three worlds

The psyche can neither be described nor understood in isolation. What is more, it does not exist in its own right. The psyche exists only as a biological organism's connection or relationship to something other than itself. This something else is nature (the natural world) and, in the case of man, culture as well.

Nature, the psyche and culture are seen here as three different "worlds" or regions of the world, inspired by K.R. Popper (1972). This means that the properties and events of each of the three worlds are qualitatively different.

The first world. Originally, there only existed physical-chemical, or inorganic matter. About five thousand million years ago in this microscopic part of the universe a handful of elements condensed to form what we call the earth. This constituted the geological, geographical, and climatological matter of the first world.

The second world. From this first world there arose life or organic matter around two-three thousand million years ago. This was the earlier second world.

At some point during the evolution of biological organisms one can reasonably ascribe a psyche to some of them. This happened long before the appearance of man, but there are no reasons here to be more precise about the exact time at which this occurred. The psyche arose as an interaction between the first world's inorganic material and the earlier second world's organic or living material. The psyche now belongs to, or is part of, the second world whose organic matter is its bridge to the first world's inorganic matter. This bridge allows the involvement of the second world in the first, although it remains at the same time an independent world.

The third world. Much later again, the cultural world, in the case of man, comes into existence (though forerunners appear amongst lower animals). Culture arose as an interchange between the first two worlds. Culture continues to exist in the form of this interchange, but has nevertheless an existence in its own right. The cultural world is therefore an independent third world.

The first, second, and third worlds. Subsequently, the human psyche consists of the second world's connections to both nature (the first world) and culture (the third world). The whole world is thus divided into these three worlds.

The nature of the psyche

To paraphrase Spencer (1881, Vol. 1), the psyche's phylogenetic nature, and with it scientific psychology's most general subject, is the correspondence between two sets of outer and inner connections, relating to the first and second worlds, respectively. Note that so far I have only mentioned the psyche as an accordance or correspondence between the first and second worlds so that the definition applies to all organisms. The third world has not yet entered into the picture.

Sciences such as physics, chemistry, geography, botany, etc. examine the co-existing connections between properties and events in biological organisms' outer material world; e.g. a fruit's colour, shape and consistency. We must assume that there exists, in principle, an infinite number of possible connections of properties and events in the external world, but that at any given time and place there will be a finite number of possible connections. The last part of this assumption is perhaps open to discussion, but for our present purpose it is of no importance. We will state these actually appearing, external and mutually connected phenomena as A + B + C + ... N.

Sciences such as physiology, biochemistry, neurology, etc. examine the co-existing connections between the properties and events in the organism's internal material world which A + B + C + ... N give rise to. We will state these internal and mutually connected phenomena as a + b + c + ... n.

Psychology, on the other hand, examines how this internal connection between a + b + c + ... n, which in one way or another corresponds to the external connection between A + B + C + ... N, arises in the organism (Spencer, 1881, Vol. 1, p. 133).

Consequently, psychology's assertions always include both the internal, mutually connected phenomena, and the external, mutually connected phenomena which the internal ones correspond to, or in other words refer to. Consequently, a psychological statement is not concerned with the immediate (direct) mutual connections between the internal physical phenomena for their own sake, nor the immediate (direct) mutual connections between the external physical phenomena for their own sake. Psychological statements are, on the other hand, exclusively concerned with the indirect correspondence between these two sets of direct material connections - (a + b + c + ... n) and (A + B + C + ... N). The psyche is no more and no less than this relationship.

The psyche is the indirect connection or meta-connection between two sets of phenomena, both of which are materially and mutually connected in a direct way. The psyche does not exist on its own, but only as this relation or indirect connection. One could describe the psyche as a middle world between the first and second worlds, but this would be incorrect, for the psyche is, and can only be, a part (or subset) of the second world. In as much as the psyche is a part of life it is material, but the psyche does amount to a new reality in the world, once it attains a reasonably developed form. The psyche is not identical to the second world's biological properties, although it has evolved from them; just as these are not identical to the first world's physical properties, although they have evolved from them. The psyche is a genuine new object in the history of the world - and consequently requires a new science. Even though there are false dualisms, there are also true ones. Something exists for itself and as something qualitatively new, while at the same time it is only existing with and as something other than itself.

Such a something is the psyche. It is something new in the relationship between the first and second world's matter. The essence of this new entity is very special in that it only exists as a relationship. A relationship is invisible and untouchable. Later I will refer to it as a 'spirit'. And yet it exists partly in or as a result of the first world's physicalness, just as the second world does, and partly in and with, or as something bound to, the second world's physicalness.

The first world is independent of, and has primacy over, the second world - including its psychological component. The second world has developed as an adaptation to the first. This is the only way one can view biological and psychological development when one uses an evolutionary perspective. However, this does not mean that the second world and its psyche is a passive product of the first world. All organisms with a psyche are self-activating. Biological life is synonomous with movement. The question of interest is, therefore, not the emergence of active life but rather why this life is restrained and controlled. For the more developed a biological organism is, the greater is the control it exerts over itself (as will be seen in the next section); not vice versa as many may believe.

The law of correspondence or development

It has been suggested that the psyche is both a new entity and a component of the second world. It is a common property of (nearly) all biological organisms. This last point means that the psyche's phylogenetic development must be seen in terms of those principles which are relevant for an understanding of biological life's development in general.

Life is the internal co-existing connections' correspondence to the external co-existing connections and the psyche's development towards ever higher forms occurs as a continuously increasing number, variety, specialisation, generalisation and complexity of the internal connections' correspondence to the external ones. The psyche, as administrator of the correspondence between the two sets of connections, gradually comes into being when the correspondences between the two sets of connections cease to be few, simple and direct (Spencer, 1881, Vol. 1, p. 294). In simple terms, one could say that the degree of both life and the psyche (as two sides of the same thing), vary with the degree of correspondence.

The following elaboration of what I will call this law of correspondence (or development) takes Spencer as its starting point but it is to a considerable extent my own reformulation.

In this section's formal definition of the psyche, one can recognise tones of dialectic materialism's view of psychic evolution as a continuously improving reflection of (correspondence to) the first world's own properties and property connections. Formulated within the framework of this theory, the definition can be briefly stated in the following way: Every biological organism above a certain primitive level is, as stated, engaged in a natural, self-activated interchange with its surroundings. The surroundings are perpetually changing in terms of geology, climate, vegetation, etc. Therefore, in order to maintain life, a species must develop new organs, limbs, etc. which possess new properties. These new properties reflect, or correspond to, or are in structural harmony with, the first world's changed properties, while at the same time they give occasion to new self-stimulated activities. The second world's changed interplay with the first world then causes new reflections and so on. Stated in Spencer's terms: in both the biological and the psychological aspects of life, its maintenance and development are two sides of the same thing (Spencer, Vol. 1, p. 319).

Throughout the whole of evolution the second world increases its active, effective control over the first world. The increase in the number, variety, precision, specialisation, generalisation and complexity of correspondences allows the organism to steadily improve its transformation and reorganisation of the external world's (in principle) infinite number of possible property-connections, into a finite number of definite, internal property-connections. As mentioned, this last point means the creation of new organs and limbs, and with these, new psychological skills of a sensory, motoric, cognitive, emotive, and social nature.

This could thus be a Spencer-inspired formulation of the thesis of mind as reflection: The objective world's own property connections (independent of the subject) become objects for the subjects' activity to a steadily increasing extent. This happens through the contrast between the merely possible and the actual control of the object. The first world's 'merely possible' section of property-connections constitutes a mere object, and maybe just a hypothetical object at that. The second world's 'actual control' of this section of the first world turns the object into an 'object for a subject'. The enhanced degree of control achieved through the increased number, precision, variety, specialisation, generalisation and complexity of correspondences leads to the subject reflecting the object in an ever more indirect way. One could say that more and more psyche fills the gap between the two sets of external and internal connections.

The indirect, active, and subjective reflection of the objective reality is in itself the psychological (Mammen, 1983, p. 209). The special human psychological, consciousness, is a highly developed version of this general psyche. Not surprisingly, consciousness possesses a number of special features which create some extremely important differences between itself and the lower versions of the general psyche. These differences can be said to be qualitative, in the sense that only human consciousness can acknowledge the objective world *as* the objective world, can act in it in a deliberate, radically conscious and thorough manner, and also write these lines about it (and in so doing become a part of its self-consciousness). In spite of these formidable differences to all other forms of mental life, consciousness has nevertheless only absorbed and reformed the characteristics of less developed life forms, it has not wiped them out (Rubinstein, 1976, p. 294).

The organism's enhancement of its correspondence (in terms of number, precision, variety, specialisation, generalisation and complexity) occurs during the systematic maintenance of the balance between *differentiation* and *integration*. Differentiation means passing from a homogeneous to a less homogeneous condition or state. Integration means passing from a condition of detached elements to one of more combined elements. Developmental balance exists in a steadily increasing differentiation of the system's parts, and a corresponding steady increase in integration. If this balance is not maintained, the organism does not develop or it develops too little, only to collapse.

In terms of the notion of mental reflection it is quite common to view the dynamics (or motor) of these chains of differentiation and integration, like Spencer does, as the second world's steadily increased control over the first world. As stated, the first world consists of an (in principle) infinite number of possible connections between properties and events. These external connections have primacy over the bio-psychic system's internal connections. These external connections are in principle changing all the time. The system's internal connections have to accommodate these changes if the species is to survive or at least develop.

The chain of continual differentiations and integrations is the structure of the process by which the naturally active bio-psychic system converts the infinite number of possible, external connections into a steadily increased number of corresponding finite, definite internal connections with certain degrees of specialisation and generalisation. In this way, the organism's mastery of an increasingly larger part of the first world becomes more and more effective.

In other words: The organisms that develop do so by reducing the external world's (in principle) infinite complexity. However, the external or first world's complexity cannot actually be reduced itself. It remains as God created it, independent of the bio-psychic system. The activity of organisms affects the first world, but obviously does not change its ontological essence of consisting of an, in principle, infinite number of possible, external connections, which remain primary to the second world's internal connections.

The reduction of the first world's complexity needs therefore to be understood as relative to the second world, i.e., as a complementary increased complexity within the bio-psychic system. It is this increased internal complexity which enhances the system's control over its outer world and thereby the species' survival capabilities during changing environmental conditions. Increased bio-psychic complexity can also be conceived of as that condition in which psyche is increasingly inserted in-between the external and internal connections.

This growth of the psyche occurs both outwardly towards the first world's connections, and inwardly towards the second world's connections. As the bio-psychic system's increased complexity allows greater control over its surroundings, its control over itself also increases. Increased self-control refers to the system's ability to regulate the second world's connection's active interchanges with the first world. This increased control over both worlds develops simultaneously, because internal control is necessarily complementary to external control. They are two aspects of the process by which the species' internal connections come into existence over a period of time in the adjustment to the external connections. As the correspondence administrator between the two sets of physical connections, the psyche's fundamental role is to be both the controller of the living organism's internal workings and of its perceptions and external functions.

The character of the internal control can be made more explicit in the following way. Some of the integrations subordinate those differentiations which they are continually following. The internal connections thus acquire a hierarchical structure in which there is (if the species develops) constantly being established higher level integrating command posts. These command posts control a number of lower levels where differentiations and integrations are continuously occurring. This is the process by which the species acquire increased complexity. Up to a point we can imagine a central nervous system's structure in this way. The same goes for the structure of the psyche which is part of the second world's materiality.

Heinz Werner (1948) has a notion of the structure of mentality along similar lines in a comparative socio/ontogenetic theory (apparently without knowledge of Spencer).

The subjective spirit

The second world thus became divided into two domains; on the one hand the organism's internal material connections, and on the other the organism's correspondence between these material connections and the material connections of the first world. This correspondence is the psyche.

The psyche is bound to individual organisms. During the course of evolution the psyche of some of these organisms become enriched by the acquisition of consciousness. I will refer to such organisms as subjects. According to the custom of ancient philosophy, the subject is that part of the psyche which gives consciousness unity, and it is therefore (literally translated from both Latin and Greek), the underlying carrier of perception, thinking, emotion and all other mental properties which we possess. The subject is the synthesis of mental unity.

Man is such a subject, presumably the only one on earth. I have earlier used the word 'subject' rather indiscriminately, but from now on it will only be employed to mean humans. I will refer to the human psyche as the subjective spirit (again according to a long standing custom). Every now and then, I may also refer to it as mind for the sake of variation.

Up to this point the evolution of the psyche has only been discussed in phylogenetic terms (i.e. in terms of all biological life). For the sake of simplicity I will call the human, phylogenetically developed correspondence between external and internal connections (between the first and second worlds) the bio-psyche.

Earlier I mentioned that at some point in human evolution the second world is supplemented by the third, or cultural world. By this I mean that to a certain extent man breaks nature's order by beginning to adjust the first world to the second. That consciousness, presumably, little by little comes into being at the same time is not important here. Man creates culture with the aid of which he begins to determine his being and history. This is known as sociogenesis.

At this point a completely new kind of external connections comes into existence, which the second world's internal connections have to correspond to (though forerunners of this exist in other creatures as well). I will call these correspondences 'cultural' as opposed to the first world's 'natural' correspondences. In addition, therefore, there develops a completely new kind of psyche within the domain of the second world which - again for the sake of simplicity - I will call the cultural-psyche.

But this is an oversimplification. Man has not suddenly acquired two psyches. Neither can the phylogenesis and sociogenesis be separated in such a distinct fashion. For the time being, however, I will not elaborate on this point.

The objective spirit

It was Popper (1972) who inspired the division of the whole world into three worlds. Popper distinguishes between: i) the world of physical objects or conditions, ii) the world of conscious states or spiritual states (or maybe, a world of behaviour dispositions) and iii) the world of objective or objectified thought contents. By this third world Popper means the human or subjective spirit's products, but he makes clear that he primarily means objective knowledge in the form of problems, critical arguments, and theoretical systems (Popper, 1972, p. 107).

By the term 'world' Popper means the entirety of that which is the case. And that which is the case can be established in the form of true statements or assertions. Subsequently, Popper is able to make specific the notion of three worlds by stating how each entity exists. According to their membership of one of the three worlds, all existing entities have a particular way of existing. They can exist as (1) physical objects and events, (2) mental states and internal episodes, and (3) symbolic product's meaning content (ibid.).

Just as the mental part of the second world has just been called the subjective spirit, one can use the term objective spirit in the case of the third world. But in contrast to the philosophy of spirit, from Hegel onwards, Popper does not consider the active spirit to have primacy (i.e. that which interprets the world that it has constituted itself). Popper maintains the primacy of the first world over both spirits and attempts to conceive the ontology of both the second and the third world by analogy with the first world (ibid.).

Considered in this way, the third world is the natural product of humanity just as a nest is for a bird, or a web is for a spider. Our tools, houses, art, etc. are basically no different when viewed ontologically (Popper, 1972, p. 113). They are, for that matter, no different to the second world's organs and limbs. Just like organs and their functions, theories and other objectified knowledge are, by way of experiment, adjustments to the first world. Theories and tools exercise influence over the first world and change it, but in this they are no different to organs, organ functions and forms of behaviour (ibid., p. 145). Organs and organ bound psychic skills, after all, come into existence with and through the second world's active mastering of, or adjustment to, the first world. This is also the case with theories, tools, and all other objectified knowledge (or in other words - the third world).

Within the domain of the third world Popper distinguishes between, on the one hand, explicit meaning-content which is embodied in the first world in the form of houses, machines, alphabets, the physical sound-waves of speech, etc., and on the other hand, implicit meaning-content which has not yet been 'discovered', i.e. has not yet become embodied in the first world's 'carrying-objects', but which already possesses inherent meaning.

These yet-to-be-realised entities of the third world show the objective spirit's independence of the subjective spirit. Of course, symbolic products come into being only as a result of the subjective spirit's activity. But despite being its product they confront the subjective spirit in the form of a persistent and impenetrable meaning which can only be illuminated through intellectual effort. The products of the human spirit return untiringly towards the human spirit in the form of problems.

In this way one can see how the meaning content of the third world can be distinguished from and acquire an independent status above the first world's physical and the second world's mental existences, respectively. It has autonomy over the first world in that it intervenes in and changes physical entities. And it has autonomy over the second world in that its knowledge-content does not consist of a single subject's thoughts and ideas. It constitutes an objective knowledge that exists both before and after the single individual's life, and therefore has an independent ontological status above the knowledge statements, convictions, and actions of individuals. It is recognition, acknowledgement, comprehension and understanding without recogniser, acknowledger, comprehender or understander (Popper, 1972, p. 109).

But even though the objective spirit is independent of the subjective spirit, it is not - according to Popper - omnipotent as Hegel claims. The objective spirit is, of course, carried only by the different subjective spirits of man (ibid. p. 125).

Habermas considers Popper's definition of the objective spirit to be rather narrow, in that it first of all serves the growth of theoretical and technical knowledge. As mentioned, Popper claims that essentially it consists of problems, theories, and critical arguments. He apparently, and one-sidedly, views the entities of the third world as science-developing (Habermas, 1981, p. 122).

Indeed, Popper also names works of art and social institutions as examples of entities in the third world, but he considers them to be no more than variants of the same type of truth-relations which are made up of the scientific study of problems (op.cit., p. 124). That is to say, they are instances of that which is the case, and about which one can therefore make true statements.

The other components of culture are thus placed in the periphery of things. Although, of course, the cultural objectifications other than those of science and technology play a large role in the understanding of man's active and social life beyond the cognitive-instrumental intercourse with the natural environment.

If one is to work with just three ontological worlds, which is sensible in light of the present level of abstraction, then they must include all existing entities. Nothing should be left without a home. This means that the third world must be filled with absolutely everything which does not belong in either the first or second worlds. I have begun this filling-up process with Habermas, but we must, in principle, name all the entities imaginable: Modes of subsistence; economic structures, visible and invisible social and political organisations and institutions, social cohesion and integration; groups, classes, subcultures; social control, norms, morals, laws; myths, rites and religions; world views, philosophies and ideologies; housing, weights and measures, telephones; technology; art, decoration, design; science; sport and festivals; knowledge, meanings, gestures, language, etc.

I have deliberately presented a completely unsorted list. This is not the place to attempt a sociological or ethnographic structuring of the third world into outlined categories with different conditions of existence, validity, and developmental histories. Habermas and many other social scientiests have already begun, and continue with, this task.

I included in my list knowledge and meanings. It goes without saying that knowledge and meaning, in a definite sense, cannot form their own sub-categories within the framework of the third world. Knowledge and meaning are part of and form the basis for all the other elements of the third world. It is, therefore, common to raise knowledge and meaning (or simply understanding), out of the third world and allocate them their own independent meta-world; that world which makes possible our understanding and comprehension of all three worlds. This meta-world, then, constitutes the recognition of all three worlds.

The elements of culture (including meaning) have, however, come into being and they undergo continual changes in exactly the same way as the rest of the third world. Therefore, when seen from a developmental perspective such as the present one, nothing existing can be moved out of that world in which it came into existence. Not even the establishment of the understanding of how understanding has come about. From an evolutionary viewpoint, meanings, language etc. therefore cannot be raised out of the sphere of the objective spirit and given independent status.

If the subjective spirit claims something else (which many of the most spiritual of spirits do), it can only be done by maintaining the impossibility of understanding the most important part of both the subjective and the objective spirits' historical progress. That is, intellect itself.

Sociogenesis

I have made a distinction between the bio-psyche and the cultural-psyche. I described the bio-psyche as the connection between the second and first worlds, and the cultural-psyche as the connection between the second and third worlds.

However, I also warned that things were not as simple as this. It is certainly quite easy to understand what is meant by bio-psyche, in principle at least. Man is an animal, and like all other animals he adjusts his internal material connections to the external ones by establishing a number of behavioural capacities in his genes. The development of these specific, gene-bound, neural and hormonal behavioural capacities is founded upon the general law of biological natural selection. At every stage of human history there thus exists a fundamental, gene-bound repertoire of cognitive, emotive, and social behavioural capacities. The unfolding of these behavioural capacities within the habitat is the second world's bio-psychic connection to the first world.

The capacity for a behaviour is, however, not the same as the actually occurring behaviour. The further we move down the phylogenetic scale, the greater the identity between behavioural capacities and actual behaviour, because behavioural capacities are instinct driven. The behavioural repertoire of the species is determined genetically. However, the further we move up the phylogenetic scale, the greater the extent to which the behavioural repertoire will contain learned behaviour. Learned behaviour depends upon the bio-psychic system's given behavioural capacity, but it also raises this capacity and therefore makes it flexible and changeable to a certain extent.

This is, of course, to a very high degree, applicable to man who is practically without instinct. This does not mean, however, that man is free from a gene-bound cognitive, emotive, and social behavioural capacity. Instincts and genetic inheritance are not identical phenomena although they are unfortunately often confused.

In the cases of animals, learning occurs directly between individual members of the species. This is, of course, also the case with man. But with man the second world is loaded with the third world. To illustrate this more clearly, we can say that learning in man is predominantly a cultural phenomenon. The third world includes everything that a man can learn, and it is also the teacher. The individual person is a pupil. The subjective spirit can create new things, and does so nearly every time it says a sentence. In this way it can teach itself, but only to the extent that it applies the objective spirit.

It is, of course, here that the cultural-psyche plays its role - the connection or relation between the second and third worlds. But this is still an over-simplification, at least from an evolutionary perspective, because from an evolutionary standpoint the human bio-psyche has come into existence as a cultural-psyche. Culture, or the third world, has played a part in the creation of the bio-psyche. It is not simply a creation of the first world.

Materially, the internal connections of the bio-psyche are localised in the nervous system's command centre - primarily the brain. Everyone is probably in agreement about this. The behavioural capacity of the bio-psyche is, therefore, to a large extent a question of the brain's volume and structure in relation to the processes of the other bodily organs; (this relationship is far from simple but I will not elaborate on it here). If we determine the minimal components of the third world as a certain amount of cooperative work sharing, social ties, and technology, then the first traces of the third world appeared, in all probability, two or maybe three to four million years ago (Katzenelson, 1983). That hominid who, at this time, stood up on two legs and began his up-right activity upon the ground possessed a brain volume comparable in size to that of a modern day chimpanzee which is only about one third the size of our brain. Two million years ago, homo faber, who is known to have used tools had a brain volume a little under half that of ours.

During the lengthy period of time since then, the human brain has evolved into its present form which contains modern man's fundamental bio-psychic behavioural capacities. The third world which existed then, increasingly became *the* specific way in which the human species adjusted to the first world. For man it is not only the first world, but the first and third worlds together which form the external world to which the internal connections adjust.

In other words, the second world is not only connected to the first world by a bio-psyche, but also by a cultural-psyche. We do not actually recognise the existence of the human species until this becomes the case.

However, this also means that the second world is not only connected to the third world by a cultural-psyche, but also by a bio-psyche. It is self-evident that man comes into contact with his third world, and not just the first world, with a bio-psychic behavioural capacity. But this should be understood in terms of the more concrete evolutionary notion that the third world's outer connections, in the course of development, are absorbed genetically into the second world's internal connections, just as the first world's external connections are. In this sense, the bio-psyche's basic cognitive, emotive, and social behavioural capacities are also a cultural inheritance, not just a natural one.

One may ask if man has two psyches. The easiest answer is that man has, of course, only one psyche, but that a distinction between the bio-psyche and the cultural psyche is practical to work with. However, a more correct answer would be that although the bio-psyche and the cultural-psyche are two aspects of the same and only psyche, they are, nevertheless, two aspects which often have so many differences that for many psychological questions there exists a real duality. In the presence of such a real duality a distinction between the bio-psyche and the cultural psyche is not only practical, but also necessary. This answer is, however, also a difficult one to justify, though I will try.

In the long (or rather, in relative terms, dramatically short) period of development from the time of man's birth between two and four million years ago until he reaches his present biological form, it is difficult to make distinctions between the biological and cultural aspects of the psyche. But after this it becomes both easier and more important to do so. We believe that after the arrival of homo sapiens sapiens 30 - 40,000 years ago, bio-psychic development of the basic behavioural capacities ceased. After this only the cultural psyche develops. The actual behaviour of this is transferred to, and learned afresh by, each subsequent generation via the third world.

Why is this imaginable? Because at this point the third world has become so productive and efficient that its external connections assume a more important position than the first world's external connections. That is, the external connections of the third world become those to which the second world's internal connections have to adapt to. The law of biological natural selection ensures the selection of those organisms which, via the correspondence administrating psyche, best adapt their internal, material connections to the geological, climatic and other changes which the external, material connections of the first world constantly go through. But when modern man (modern in a biological sense) makes his entry upon history's scene he does so with a very efficient third world at his disposal. This third world is a flexible buffer between the second and first worlds. Now, when the external, material connections of the first world change, the second world no longer adjusts its internal, material connections in tune with these changes. Instead, man adapts his third world to the changes in the first world.

As mentioned, the psyche is inserted between the external and internal material connections. The psyche divides the second world into a spiritual and a material part. The psyche's phylogenetic evolution consists of a continual injection of more and more subjective spirit in-between the external and internal matter. With the beginning of the earliest sociogenesis two - four million years ago the psyche itself is divided into a subjective and an objective spirit (Katzenelson, 1983), and from now on also injects more objective spirit in-between the external and internal matter.

In other words, the second world begins to actively change the third world every time the first world's changes demand new adaptations, and bit by bit man also begins to change the third world without such direct demands for change from the first world - an activity that now has no end. The internal, material connections of the second world subsequently adapt to both (i) the first world's spontaneous changes, and (ii) those changes in the first world which the constantly growing objective spirit of the third world has caused. Both forms of adaptation become a genetically built-in part of the second world.

Accordingly, our notion is that at some point in time the second world will have inserted so much, and so efficient, third world in-between itself and the physical first world that the changes in the first world no longer have any biological evolutionary effect upon man's internal, material connections. The shield has become so thick that the biological laws of natural selection no longer apply. When the third world becomes so productive and efficient that it is, to a large extent, able to master the first world, the second world loses all evolutionary-based reasons for changing its internal, material connections. It changes the third world instead. Hence, from now on it is only the internal, cultural-psychic connections of the second world that change.

Thus, one can assume that the basic cognitive, emotive and social behavioural capacities of the bio-psyche have not changed since the arrival of homo sapiens sapiens 30-40,000 years ago - the year 0. There is nothing accidental or random about this date, but this point will not be taken up in the present discussion. Genetic changes certainly occur during the adaptations of future generations to the first world, for example - the development of racial characteristics in terms of colour, body shape and size, bloodtype, etc., but the basic cognitive, emotive and social behavioural capacities of the bio-psyche are universal and invariable. Subsequently, it is only the cultural-psychic behaviour which changes in accordance with local demands, or relative time and place.

One could throw more light on this story by introducing a distinction between cultural-psyche 1 and cultural-psyche 2 as well as between sociogenesis 1 and sociogenesis 2. Cultural-psyche 1 appears at the same time as man's first sociogenetic origins two - four million years ago. It achieves a close connection to, or becomes one with, the bio-psyche. Cultural-psyche 2 on the other hand first appears with the second sociogenesis of man which is often viewed as identical to the beginnings of a reasonably extensive and complex, and here by efficient and productive, third world.

Consequently, cultural-psyche 1 ceases to exist in that it becomes part of or is absorbed by the bio-psyche. Today there exists, however, two genuine aspects of the psyche. There exists both an unchangeable and universal bio-psyche, and there exists a changeable and local cultural-psyche (cultural-psyche 2).

Sociogenesis and the problem of development

We can now define the area of interest of human psychology (as Leontiev does, to give a classic example) as the study of the transitions between the three levels of man, in as much as these interact within the concrete activities of life (Leontiev, 1978, pp. 142-143): (1) The biological level at which man appears as a natural creature, (2) the psychological level at which man can engage in activity regulated by the psyche, and (3) the social level at which man is realising objective social conditions.

According to Leontiev, these levels can neither be reduced into each other, nor viewed as existing one above the other in a hierarchical fashion. One can better understand the relationships involved by considering the ontogenetic development of man: When a baby comes into the world the first adjustments that are made are at the biological level. These biological adaptations are then transformed by the other levels. The biological level does not then cease to function. Rather, the biological adaptations begin to realise higher levels of activity, and the extent of their contribution to these higher levels depends upon each particular developmental stage. The task is therefore to examine the possibilities or limits which they entail (ibid.). The main principle involved in the mutual relationships of these levels is that at any given time the currently higher level will always be dominant, but at the same time it can only be realised with the help of the lower levels and is, therefore, dependent upon these (ibid.). This logic also applies to the psychic development of the species.

This is a fairly common notion of the principle of psychic development, especially within the tradition of dialectic materialism. It is also the correct view, without which development could not be understood. There remains, however, the question of whether this notion is more appropriate for the ontogenetic development of the individual than it is for the phylogenesis and sociogenesis of mankind. It is a question whether psychological development, in the strictest meaning of the term, has anything at all to do with the progression of mankind after the year 0. Maybe one should be talking here about unfolding rather than development. The following represents perhaps a controversial opinion on these issues, but I believe that it should nevertheless be considered seriously.

The cognitive, emotive, and social behavioural-capacities of the bio-psyche are not capable of development in any material sense. By the end of biological development the bio-psyche is fully established and determined. On the other hand, the behavioural-capacities of man are variable and they are capable of expansion. More and more of them expand, becoming increasingly comprehensive, abundant, varied and complex. The behavioural capacities are capable of acquiring extra, new aspects which can then be synthesised in higher level command posts. This unfolding is the actual cultural-psychic behaviour of individuals, groups and races at any given time and place. It can undoubtedly be called development and it occurs in proportion to (but not exactly proportional in a straightforward way) what the culture of the local time and place demands and allows. It is in other words an enterprise in which every new born individual must begin from the beginning.

But the nature of man must be species-determined, not individuals-determined. Once again this means that it must be determined by natural history and not cultural history. Otherwise mankind would have no essence, but would simply consist of about 5 thousand million organisms going around pretending to resemble each other. The essence of man must therefore exist in a bio-psyche which is no longer capable of development. The given local culture cannot place any developmental demands upon the bio-psyche. On the other hand, the bio-psyche may require something of the culture whereupon the culture both demands and permits self-expansion and variation in the form of an increasingly copious cultural-psyche (within the limits of the bio-psyche).

To call this increasingly copious expansion of the cultural-psyche development would certainly be consistent with the meaning of the term, and this development affects each form of the bio-psyche. The various forms of the bio-psyche are therefore different from one culture to the next. The differences may be small, but nevertheless they are there. Conversely, even large differences do not change that which forms the basis of the bio-psyche.

Even though we are discussing the whole of the psyche's development in general it is very important to be able to make the distinction between the bio-psyche and the cultural-psyche, no matter how rigid and undialectic it sounds. A distinction needs to be made between the bio-psyche's natural-historical development and its termination on the one hand (although this has also come into existence as a first cultural-psyche), and the second cultural-psyche's further cultural-historical development and continued developmental capability on the other hand. There are at least two reasons for this distinction.

Firstly, the increasingly rich and varied expansion of the cultural-psyche complemented by cultural expansion does not necessarily always benefit the bio-psyche. For example, the reflections of the cultural-psyche can drain or paralyse the bio-psyche's sovereign manifestations of life, as Hamlet would say.

The second reason is that the lack of this distinction could lead to dangerous forgetfulness. It is of utmost importance to be able to understand man's cultural nature as one thing and man's natural culture as something else. For the demands which the bio-psyche places upon each particular culture are much more compulsory than the demands made by the cultural-psyche upon each biological individual.

In spite of this there is no use in diversifying the second world's volume and content. It consists of the bio-psyche and the cultural-psyche, which are one and undivisible. Every psyche (or mental phenomenon) contains both aspects. It is unavoidably misleading to divide the psyche into two separate regions. The twin aspects of nature and culture are, however, real. Man is both a creature of nature and a creature of culture. As a creature of nature he has become cultured and that is why his natural essence is historical. Conversely, his history has come about through nature and that is why his history is natural (Marx & Engels, 1976).

Along with Leontiev and others we can say that at any given time the higher levels of activity play a dominant role in development. They are the locomotive of development and the motor is culture's complex of different constellations of production, reproduction, organisation, etc. But this development consists of the bio-psyche's cultural-psychic expansion. Therefore, the higher levels of activity are not dominating in the long run. It would be dangerously rash to believe they were.

The (cultural-)psyche expands in different ways. But it is the same (bio-) psyche which expands. Beyond that it is obvious that the psyche behaves in this way, it is also a beautiful thought, I believe. If we paid a little more attention to it, then quite a few things around us would presumably appear in a different light.

The correspondence between the first and the second, and between the second and the third worlds

The relationship between the second and first worlds was considered earlier. The second world has correspondence connections with the first world. The psyche is the spiritual correspondence administrator between the external and the internal material connections. The more developed a species' psyche is, the more correctly will its internal connections be adapted to the first world's external connections.

What then is the relationship between the second world and the third world? In principle, it is the same, for as has been mentioned, the third world is, at any given point in time, just as objective and independent of each and every individual of the second world as is the first world. This is so regardless of the fact that it is the second world which has created the third world, (which, of course, does not apply in the case of the first world). Therefore, the more accurately the individual's internal connections are adapted to the third world's external connections, or the greater the extent to which they reflect the third world's external connections, the more developed will the individual's psyche be.

Consequently, the second world has, in principle, the same relationship to the third world as it has to the first world. However, there are two important qualifying aspects which should be noted.

Firstly, the developmental relationship between the second world and the first world is, in principle, of a species dependent character. Phylogenetically, it is only meaningful to talk about lower or higher development of a whole species. In contrast, the developmental relationship between the second and the third worlds is of an individual character. When considered sociogenetically it is only meaningful to talk about lower or higher development of an individual's psyche in relation to the historically specific or particular local character of the third world. This is so - regardless of the fact that it is, of course, the local third world which plays the decisive role in determining which individual cultural-psychological development that possibly can occur.

Secondly, it would be unfortunate to use the term adaptation or adjustment, as a matter of course, in the same way for the connection between the second and third worlds as for the connection between the second and first worlds. For there is an important difference between the two sets of connections despite the similarities. From a historical perspective the second world is not simply 'adapted' or 'adjusted' to the third world. This appears to be the case in a time stopping single frame snapshot. More or less at least, but certainly more than less. Otherwise the individual could not exist. Each man is obliged to take over certain fundamental parts of that third world which exist at his time and place. If he does not, he dies. But when one considers a developmental period in terms of the species, it is, of course, the second world that not only carries the third world but which has also created it, and it is from the second world the third world is re-created and developed every single second.

It is a small but nevertheless important point, for it is here that the designation of the third world as objective spirit can lead one astray. And it has, indeed, done so throughout the history of thought. It has led to idealistic thinking - so-called objective idealism. That this thought is objective means that it correctly understands the third world as independent of the second world. But that it is idealistic also means that it incorrectly views the objective spirit as governing over its own domain, above the heads of the second world - to use, in this context, an apt expression.

The third world is ultimately carried, created, recreated and developed by the second world during the latter's active, practical and efficient interaction with the first world. In spite of the fact that the objective spirit is at any given time objective and independent of the subjective spirit, it is - seen in terms of a historical, developmental period - no more than a product of the subjective spirit's practical and efficient activity upon earth. The objective spirit is the spirit of the third world. It is not, in addition, an all-embracing world-spirit.

Therefore, it is unnecessarily confusing to refer to the second world's connection to the third world as a mere adaptation, in the same way as one more reasonably can with respect to the second world's connection to the first world. The notion of adaptation all too easily leads to a mistaken view of the second world's existence as being secondary to the third world.

The correspondence between the first world and the third world

The previous section was concerned with the correspondence between the second world and the other two worlds.

Can we close the triangle by establishing a correspondence between the first world and the third world? The answer is no; at least not directly. The third world exists, just as the second world does, **in** the first world. But there is not and cannot be a direct connection between the first world and the third.

Bird's nests are only connected with the first world by the bird's activity. The same applies to man's third world. The objective spirit is lifeless, regardless of how lively it might behave. Only nature or matter can have life. The non-matter of the second world, the subjective spirit, also has life. But this is only because it is bound to the second world's organic matter and in this way it is, of course, part of the first world.

As is known, the subjective spirit also disappears with death. However, the objective spirit is pure spirit and contrary to common belief it is as such lifeless, although it does not disappear with the death of the individual's soul. It can do nothing independently. It can neither establish connections in an outward direction nor in an inward direction. The objective spirit lives only when the subjective spirit animates it.

The third world exists through and is carried by the second world. The objective spirit is, indeed, independent in relation to the subjective spirit but it is not self-sustained. It is tiresome but it cannot be said often enough. The first and second worlds can interact, and the second and the third worlds can interact. Thus the second world can interact with each of the other two worlds. The vibrant, breathing individual is at the centre of things. But the third world can only interact with the first world via the second world. The third world's influence on the first world, which is today enormous, always goes by way of the second world (Popper, 1972, p. 155).

However, through its direct connections to both the first and the third worlds, the second world does establish an indirect connection between the other two worlds. During the course of development, both before and after the year zero, the second world establishes such indirect connections between the other two worlds to a steadily increasing extent. There is no limit to these connections but they remain indirect.

On the other hand, attempting to bypass the second world and suggesting the existence of a direct connection between the first and third worlds is, as stated, a case of idealistic fantasy.

Short-circuiting, inflation and objective idealism

As has been stated, there does not exist a direct connection between the third world and the first world because the objective spirit is only carried by the subjective spirit. Only the individuals of the second world interact directly with the first world. The third world is only indirectly connected to the first world.

The assertion here is that innumerable philosophers, humanists, and social theorists short-circuit this indirect circuit by establishing a direct connection between the third and first worlds, as a rule without realising it or wanting to realise it. In this one witnesses the appearance of the objective spirit in one or another variation of that catastrophic philosophy known as objective idealism.

What is it that these objective idealists do, each in their own way? Firstly, they uncouple the bio-psychic part of the second world's connections to both the first and third worlds. Secondly, they generally underplay or completely ignore the connection between the second and first worlds, whereby the complimentary connection between the second and third worlds is overemphasised. Thirdly, the last connection is held to go in only one direction, i.e. from the third world to the second. This means that the third world is inflated. It swells up and occupies or swallows up the second world. The second world is no longer seen either as the creator of or the carrier of the third world. Rather, the relationship is reversed.

Whether one is aware of it or not, the second world is in this way diluted or abolished as the active and efficient carrier and generator of all the connections between all three worlds. There is established a direct and therefore short-circuited connection between the first and the third worlds, regardless of how many times one must cross oneself at the thought, and regardless of the fact that it is imaginary, due to it being an ontological impossibility. Furthermore, this direct connection also has a tendency to be uni-directional, the direction being from the third world to the first. Thus, even the first world is occupied by the third world.

The short-circuit necessarily follows. How else can the third world be connected to the first, which it must be in some way or another, when the second world only exists within and through one of the third world's entities (usually language). That is to say that the second world's existence is without its own evolutionary origins, historical nature and natural history. It is thus not the creator and carrier of the third world, but at any given time and place merely an occupied part of the third world.

The inflation and short-circuiting arising from objective idealism belong to those philosophical catastrophies that can lead to damage in nature. These, however, are left unnamed here, as they are spelt out on the daily front-page.

Summary

The human psyche consists of the connection between (1) nature, (2) the human organism, and (3) culture. Nature is the first world, the human organism and psyche is the second world, and culture is the third world.

The phylogenetic nature of the psyche consists in the correspondence between two sets of physical connections; one external (the first world) and one internal (the second world).

The development of the psyche, like the development of all biological life, consists in a continual increase in the number, variety, precision, specialisation, generalisation and complexity of the internal connections' correspondence to or reflection of the external connections. This increase occurs during the systematic maintenance of the balance between differentiation and integration which occurs at increasingly higher integrated levels of complexity.

The phylogenetic correspondence between the first and second worlds is called the bio-psyche. The sociogenetic correspondence between the second and third worlds is called the cultural psyche. Together and in the case of man they are called the subjective spirit.

According to Popper the third world consists of objectified thought content. This is called the objective spirit, and it has autonomy in relation to the subjective spirit but is not sustained without it. The third world must contain everything that is not contained within the first two worlds; e.g. all social, technological, and symbolic entities.

The bio-psyche and the cultural-psyche developed as one from two to four million years ago. Around 40,000 years ago their paths departed and only the cultural-psyche remained capable of development.

The relationship between the second world and the third world has in principle the same correspondence character as does the relationship between the second world and the first world, apart from the facts that this relationship only applies to individuals and not to species, and that it involves a form of acquisition rather than adaptation.

On the other hand, the third world is only indirectly connected with the first world. The only connection of these two worlds is via the second world. Many social scientists have inflated the third world and established a direct and short-circuited connection between it and the first world. This implies that both the second and the first worlds are swallowed up by the third world.

References

Habermas, J. (1981). *Theorie des kommunikativen Handelns 1-2*. Frankfurt/M.

Katzenelson, B. (1983). "Træk af åndens og sjælens historie, I: Ånden". (Features of the history of the mind and soul. Part I: The mind). *Psyke & Logos, 4*, 209-243.

Leontiev, A.N. (1975). *Activity, consciousness, and personality*. New Jersey.

Mammen, J. (1983). *Den menneskelige sans*. (The human sense). Copenhagen.

Marx, K. & Engels, F (1976). *The German ideology*. Moscow.

Popper, K.R. (1972). *Objective knowledge: An evolutionary approach*. Oxford.

Rubinstein, S.L. (1976). *Væren og bevidsthed*. (Being and consciousness). Copenhagen.

Spencer, H. (1855). *The principles of psychology, Vols. 1-2*, (3rd ed.). London, 1881.

Werner, H. (1948). *Comparative psychology of mental development*. New York, 1961.

The Relationship between Subject and Object from the Perspective of Activity Theory

Jens Mammen

1   Introduction

The general concept of activity and the concept of activity in psychology

The theme to be discussed here has been a recurrent one in the discussions I have shared in recent years with Henrik Poulsen, Niels Engelsted and Lars Hem. It involves an attempt to understand the specific meaning of the concept of activity which, as the name suggests, is the central concept in the Soviet psychologist A.N. Leontiev's (1903-1979) so-called theory of activity[1].

I will start with a general introduction (sections 1-3) and then go on to analyse the concept of activity in psychology (sections 4-5). Next, I will consider the assumptions and implications of this activity concept with respect to the understanding of nature or matter in general (sections 6-7), that is, questions that are relevant to the subject matter of other sciences including philosophy.

Finally (sections 8-10), I will return to psychology and consider the possibilities of reformulating the concept of activity, so as to make more clear its general content with respect to the world's organisation in general, and its *specific* content concerning psychology.

It is, of course, a very ambitious enterprise and I claim in no way to possess a final solution. In the short space available here it will only be possible to present suggestions and problem formulations.

On the other hand, I believe that there is an urgent need to understand what assumptions and implications the concept of activity involves outside of psychology's own field.

Psychology may be seen as a figure on a ground. This ground is made up of other sciences such as philosophy, physics, chemistry, biology and sociology. The possibility of making the concepts of psychology more precise depends upon which ground one is standing on. Among other things the problems which many have in understanding or accepting the meaning and implications

---

[1]   See A.N. Leontiev *Problems of the Development of the Mind* (1981) and *Activity, Consciousness, and Personality* (1978).

of activity theory within psychology have their basis in what I will call a mechanistic understanding of the world in general. This mechanistic understanding comes from outside of psychology. This implicit understanding of the world needs to be made explicit, to be refuted and then replaced by an alternative before we can come any further in the discussion of the conceptual foundations of psychology.

2   The concept of activity and dialectical materialism

Before embarking upon a closer analysis of the concept of activity I would first like to take into account a possible objection.

An obvious objection to my project is that Leontiev himself has already stated the extent to which the concept of activity is bound up with one's understanding of the world and of the different sciences. He has done this by basing the activity concept within the methodological and philosophical framework of dialectical materialism and marxism. According to this objection there should not be any need for a further explication and discussion of the activity concept's and activity theory's general philosophical foundation.

This is an understandable objection, but it also shows why the concept and theory of activity might not have achieved the success they deserve. Dialectical materialism and marxism are certainly a big mouthful to swallow. However, I do believe that to a much greater extent today than during Marx' and Engels' time it is possible to make more precise and concrete that part of dialectical materialism that primarily constitutes the philosophy behind activity theory. Finally, I am convinced that such a clarification includes new formulations and further theoretical developments of this philosophy.

Dialectical materialism as a conceptual framework may at first appear to be pure philosophy and methodology. In terms of a widespread understanding this means that it has an a priori or dogmatic character.

However, I am of the opinion (cf. Mammen, 1986) that in the long run there are no philosophical questions in this sense, and presumably dialectical materialism would also maintain this. It is correct that behind actual scientific knowledge there lies philosophical opinion and understanding. But it is also correct that behind philosophical views there lies actual scientific knowledge and other experience. Philosophy as such is not an a priori science. I will claim that there are no a priori sciences. Not even logic or mathematics ought to be described as a priori sciences.

At any given time during the course of history questions may appear to be a priori or "purely philosophical". But in the long run the questions are bit by bit transferred to real scientific questions that lead to their practical settlement. This process is, of course, a long one, and I do not believe that we can accomplish this process for all current philosophical questions including problems of the conceptual framework of dialectical materialism. So I will desist from any attempt to either "boil it down" to eternal and unchangeable fundamental principles or "translate" its assertions into more immediately real scientific questions.

I will let dialectical materialism stand as a profound but unfinished generalisation of scientific knowledge for which you have very good arguments, and can hope for still better ones in the future.

3 The psychological concept of activity as a possible paradigm for other sciences

Instead of a more general philosophical treatment of the relationship between dialectical materialism and psychology I will use the concept of activity or activity theory as a kind of probe which I will place into the conceptual fields of psychology, philosophy, physics, etc. in order to see how it relates to each. In this way I can perhaps make a contribution to the cohesion that exists between the various sciences and which we cannot do without.

In *Activity, Consciousness, and Personality* (1978, pp. 141-143) Leontiev discusses the problem of the connections and "transitions" between the different "levels" of understanding of man, which are abstracted in the different sciences, (e.g. physics, chemistry, biology, psychology, and sociology). This problem is of central importance to psychology.

But maybe this fundamental psychological problem, as illuminated by an examination of the activity concept, is also able to make concrete and explain more general and fundamental questions concerning the world's and matter's organisation. Maybe it is now the turn of psychology to make a contribution to our understanding of the world, just as it was physic's turn in the 17th century.

The developments in physics in the 17th century did not simply entail a revolution within physics itself, they also ushered in and legitimated the impressive mechanistic world view of the Late Renaissance and Age of Enlightenment[2].

Maybe a corresponding revolutionary development within psychology is on its way. Such an optimistic view has been expressed by Niels Engelsted (Engelsted, 1989).

In other words, we will see if the concept of activity involves not only a specific understanding of psychology and its subject matter, but also a more or less implicit, specific and fertile understanding of the field around and under psychology.

---

[2]   Kurt Lewin (1931) has described this revolution in his famous article on Aristotelian and Galilean modes of thought in psychology.

Jens Mammen

4   The concept of activity and Leontiev's theory of activity

I use the term "concept of activity" instead of "activity theory" because I do not intend to discuss activity theory in its entirity here. I have in other contexts attempted to deal with activity theory in a broader sense (Mammen, 1983; 1986).[3]

I will focus here upon a central feature of Leontiev's definition of "activity" as given in *Activity, consciousness, and personality* (1978).

The feature in question is Leontiev's contrast of his "three-stage schema of analysis" or so-called "trinomial formula" with the traditional and more mechanical "two-stage schema of analysis", or so-called "binomial formula". Correspondingly, Leontiev contrasts the concept of activity with what he and the Soviet psychologist D.N. Usnadse call "the postulate of directness " (Leontiev, 1978, p. 47). Along with Dreier (1981, p. 11) one could perhaps say that Leontiev's activity concept implies a "postulate of indirectness".

I will briefly explain what Leontiev means by this three-stage schema of analysis and his "postulate of indirectness". I will take the opportunity, however, to state that I am not quite happy with Leontiev's terminology, since I think it is directing attention away from the essential point. Therefore, I will (in section 5) attempt to reformulate Leontiev's definition.

But let us first see what Leontiev himself has to say.

Leontiev takes as his starting point the famous First Thesis on Feuerbach[4] by Marx, an extract of which reads:

"The chief defect of all previous materialism (that of Feuerbach included) is that thing (Gegenstand), reality, sonsousness are conceived only in the form of the *object, or of contemplation, sensous human activity, practice*, not subjectively. Hence, in contradistinction to materialism, the *active* side was set forth abstractly by idealism - which, of course, does not know real, sensous activity as such. Feuerbach wants sensous objects, really distinct from conceptual objects, but he does not conceive human activity itself as *objective* (gegenständliche) activity ..." (Marx & Engels, 1976, p. 615). (Marx' italics).

---

[3]   The reader is also referred to discussions of this theory by Henrik Poulsen (1982; 1985), Ole Dreier (1974; 1981; 1983), Niels Engelsted (1984; 1989), Benny Karpatschof (1984); Erik Schultz (1988) and a number of other Danish psychologists, primarily in the journals *Psyke & Logos* and *Udkast*.

[4]   cf. Niels Engelsted's contribution to this book.

Here Marx contrasts mechanistic materialism's view of the subject as *passively* receiving or contemplating the *external* object with idealism's view of the subject as *actively* creating its object in the subject's own *internal* form. As a dialectical sublation[5] of this contrast, Marx establishes his own dialectical materialistic view of the subject as active and practically effectual in its connections with the external objects.

Leontiev transfers this to psychology. On the one hand we have the modern versions of mechanistic materialism, which, according to Leontiev, include behaviourism and "cybernetic" psychology and their theories of man as a passive recipient of the environment's stimuli or input. Regardless of diverse internal complications within the individual the basic conception is that of a passive two-stage schema of analysis: External stimulation of the individual and the individual's reaction to stimulation.

On the other hand we have the modern psychological versions of idealism; the "science of the spirit" and "mentalistic" psychology (Leontiev, 1978, p. 45), but Leontiev makes less of these. His main interest is in the more mechanistic, and natural science inspired psychologies, especially cybernetic psychology (in our day - "cognitive science") which he rightly accuses of reductionism and which he generally polemises energetically against.

Just like Marx', Leontiev's activity concept is intended to sublate (aufheben) the opposition between the two one-sided views of the subject-object relationship - that of mechanistic materialism and that of idealism.

Leontiev dissociates himself from mechanistic materialism by replacing the object's direct determination of the subject. Instead, the subject's object-oriented activity becomes a "middle stage" between the object and the subject. Thus, the relationship between the subject and the object becomes indirect or "three-staged". Or as Leontiev (1978, p. 50) says:

"Thus, in psychology the following alternative was devised: either to keep the basic binomial formula: action of the object $= = >$ change in ongoing condition of the subject (or which is essentially the same thing, the formula $S = = > R$), or to devise a trinomial formula including a middle link ("middle term") - the activity of the subject and, correspondingly, conditions, goals, and means of that activity - a link that mediates the ties between them."

---

[5] "Sublation" (and the corresponding verb "sublate") is here used as a translation of Hegel's and Marx' concept of "Aufhebung" ("aufheben", respectively), which means a creative synthesis of two opposed conceptions that conserves their relative content of truth and at the same time denies their false or over-inclusive generalisations.

The distance to idealism is stressed to a slightly lesser extent, but occurs partly by the assertion that the object, which becomes the object of a subject through the subject's activity, at the same time also exists independently of the subject. It has its "independent properties, connections and relations" (Leontiev, 1978, p. 53).

But these definitions are hardly precise enough to make the concept of activity immune to the reductionism of for example "cybernetic psychology".

Leontiev defines activity's content as human life itself which he specifies in the following way (1978, p. 50):

> "But what is human life? It is that totality, more precisely, that system of activities replacing one another. In activity there does take place a transfer (transition, transformation, JM's comment) of an object into its subjective form, into an image; also in activity a transfer of activity into its objective results, into its products, is brought about. Taken from this point of view, activity appears as a process in which mutual transfers between the poles "subject-object" are accomplished. "In production the personality is objectivised; in need (i.e. consumption, JM's comment) the thing is subjectivised", noted Marx.[6]

Leontiev is right, of course, but is it fully convincing? What are these "transfers" (transitions, transformations) that the mechanistic materialists are unable to grasp with their primitive mechanistic concepts? I expect that the most stubborn of them would claim that if they can be precisely explained then they can undoubtedly be simulated with a machine.

Leontiev experiments with more exact formulations of activity's special "circular structure" (1978, p. 53), but in my view, without achieving a conceptual clarification that is basically different from corresponding cybernetic notions of complicated feed-back mechanisms.

I believe that one of Leontiev's difficulties is that he uses a single definition for two purposes. On the one hand he deliniates dialectical materialism's world view from mechanistic materialism and idealism, and on the other hand he deliniates that activity which is unique to living subjects and especially the human subject. He thus says indirectly, on the one hand, that the "three-stage schema of analysis" and the "postulate of indirectness" are not applicable to inanimate nature; almost, in fact, that inanimate nature is passive and mechanically materialistic. On the other hand he is indirectly saying that life's special feature is that it fits with the principles of dialectical materialism.

---

6   In *Grundrisse*. See Marx, 1973, p. 89).

This resembles, to a disturbing degree, Rubinstein's similar attempt in *Sein und Bewusstsein* (Rubinstein, 1973) to define the object of human psychology as being practically identical with the marxist theory of knowledge (cf. Mammen, 1983, pp. 157 and 163).

5   Activity as (real) abstraction

To untangle these threads one must on the one hand expose the fundamental dialectical materialistic claim concerning material activity which forms part of the activity concept, and on the other hand uncover the special claims concerning the activity of life and mental activity which also lay hidden within the concept - including the assertion concerning that which is specific to human activity.

The key to this task can be found in Leontiev's own work.

In connection with his discussion of the relationship between activity and consciousness (1978, p. 79), it is precisely the postulate of directness which Leontiev contrasts with his own opinion - "that the psychic image even from the very beginning "is related" to a reality that is external with respect to the brain of the subject and is not projected into the external world but more likely is extracted from it. Of course, when I speak of "extracting", this is only a metaphor."

In an article on "Psychology of the perceptual image" (1982) Leontiev uses the same expression - "extract" (in German - "herausholen"), and furthermore he does so in clear sympathy with J.J. Gibson's concept "pick-up" (cf. Mammen, 1986, p. 185).

The point here is that activity (in this case man's), through its special form, practically abstracts or "extracts" its objects from the world's multiplicity. Depending upon its form and direction, the activity brings the subject into contact with different aspects and levels of reality, which then asserts itself upon the subject.

The various forms of matter and their infinite number of properties first become abstracted into objects through the process of activity.

The keyword here is "abstraction". Activity is abstraction, or maybe one should say: Activity is "real-abstraction" so as not to confuse it with thought-abstraction which is a special case.

I think Leontiev would agree to this, and it might have given him an advantage in the discussion with the so-called "cybernetic theorists" (e.g. cognitivists) who basically only concern themselves with an already abstracted world - a world of "oven-ready" or "post hoc" objects in relation to man's experience.

My first assertion then is that *activity is abstraction*.

I am more doubtful as to the extent Leontiev would agree to my next assertion, namely, that *in this fundamental sense all matter is active*.

To go the whole length I will assert that this general activity in matter is a precondition for the special form of activity found in living activity, mental activity, and especially human activity or experience.

My assertion is actually analogous with Lenin's claim that there must be a general reflective capacity in matter as a basis for the special mental reflection (Lenin, 1972, pp. 37, 46, 92)[7].

I will defend the assertion that activity, viewed as "real abstraction", is a property of matter and not just of life's activity, in the following sections (sections 6-7).

To defend such an assertion is, of course, not easy for me as a psychologist. I am neither a physicist nor a chemist, and one might therefore feel that I should refrain from making this type of claim. In fact, I would prefer not to, but feel forced into this discussion.

As I have mentioned earlier, psychology is a figure on a ground that consists partly of the natural sciences. And it actually appears that there is a more or less implicit view of nature in the psychological theories that I discuss here (e.g. so-called "cybernetic" psychology and apparently Leontiev's psychology as well) that is problematical, and which indirectly determines the definitions of psychology's basic concepts, e.g. the concept of activity.

The view of nature then is already part of the picture, and may therefore just as well be placed on the agenda - the sooner the better.

6   The concept of activity in the natural sciences

I am fortunate that certain natural scientists have pre-empted me by raising the question of what implications one's view of nature has for the understanding of life and man, and conversely, what life's and human culture's reality demand of the understanding of nature.

Here I will draw attention to the Russian-born, Belgian Nobel Prize winner in chemistry, Ilya Prigogine and his book *Order out of chaos* (1984), co-written with Isabelle Stengers.

One of Prigogine and Stengers' main tasks is to demonstrate how aged and inadequate the still commonly held mechanistic view of nature is. In a

---

[7]   See also Mammen (1983, p. 156) and Niels Engelsted's discussion of the question (1989, volume II, p. 72f), and finally Prigogine and Stengers (1984, p. 82).

brilliant historical review they show what a completely dominating role the classical, Newtonian view of the world as a deterministic machine has played up to the present, not just with regard to our understanding of nature, but also in philosophy and the human and social sciences. One has, therefore, had to choose between subjugation under the all-devastating power of mechanism, or ignoring nature, with the consequence of alienating man from his natural background.

The authors point out, for example, the schism between our view of nature as something that moves without changing or developing, and our view of history as involving radical change and as something that cannot be turned back.

But that which is most relevant to my present purpose is probably the authors' demonstration of mechanism's inadequacy within natural science's own central subject area.

The view of nature which they present as an alternative is a picture of a world undergoing qualitative change and development. Prigogine and Stengers talk plainly of an "evolutionary paradigm" (1984, p. 297f). Under certain conditions in which matter is in particular states of instability, there can arise new forms of matter through a process of *self-organisation*. If subsequent conditions allow, these new forms of matter may survive. Depending on chance fluctuations a *selection* (pp. 16, 276), or a *choice* (p. 160) occurs, and matter attains a new order upon the ruins of the old. Prigogine and Stengers talk here about "bifurcations" or about "symmetry-breaking" in which there arise new qualities - *new dimensions* in reality.

There are many examples of the appearance of such new qualities in the development of the universe. For example, the appearance of substance (matter and anti-matter) after the very first seconds of the universe's existence. Moreover, the unequal amounts of matter and anti-matter is a good example of broken symmetry.

The creation of elements from elementary particles and of the chemical connections even later in the earlier stages of the universe's development are also examples of the appearance of completely new qualities or dimensions of reality.

But there is one of these qualitative transformations that Prigogine and Stengers are particularly interested in. It is a property that becomes attached to ensembles or systems of particles. It is a completely new property of such systems, one which did not exist in the individual particles, namely, the system's entropy or degree of "disorder", a concept that is connected with the concept of heat and which is studied in thermodynamics, but which is not completely the same as heat.

The peculiar thing with entropy is that it is a magnitude that in an isolated system can only increase - it can never decrease. This is contained in the famous second law of thermodynamics or entropy theorem. The radically new element in this theorem in relation to the mechanical laws (both Newtonian mechanics and quantum mechanics), is that time is given a direction so to speak. The mechanical laws hold a neutral position with regard to the direction of time. A travelling system that follows mechanical laws, including the laws of quantum mechanics, will also follow them by travelling backwards in time.

The observational situation in quantum mechanics is, on the other hand, irreversible. According to Prigogine and Stengers this is connected with the fact that a change occurs between the microscopic and macroscopic (ensemble) levels, and this last level cannot be derived from the formalism of quantum mechanics (see also Nørretranders, 1985, p. 336).

The entropy theorem introduces an asymmetry in time that was not present at the mechanistic level. Ensembles of particles follow laws that cannot be derived from mechanics. Indeed, Ludwig Boltzmann, who developed a statistical theory of thermodynamics, tried to explain the entropy theorem in terms of mechanical principles. But, it is said that when he discovered his explanation was equally applicable if the system travelled backwards in time, he became so frustrated that he committed suicide. This was in 1906 (Prigogine and Stengers, 1984, p. 253).

Prigogine and Stengers also try themselves to explain the entropy theorem by using the concept of information. As far as I can see, their explanation is one concerning probabilities understood as subjective expectations and this solution is not better than Boltzmann's. My guess would be that the information concept has to be derived from the entropy concept rather than vice versa. Let us hope that if Prigogine and Stengers reach the same conclusion they take it better than Boltzmann[8]!

The interesting point concerning entropy then, is firstly, that it implies that nature's development has fundamentally irreversible features. Secondly, entropy plays a decisive role in the set of conditions which Prigogine and Stengers put forward as being involved in the appearance of new self-organised order (of qualitatively new matter) - including the appearance of life. It is on this point that Prigogine and Stengers are most comprehensive and enlightening, but I will not go into details about this here[9].

---

[8]   The English physicist, Stephen Hawking (1988), expresses the same opinion concerning the relationship between information and entropy as I do here.

[9]   cf. Niels Engelsted's contribution to this book.

The crucial thing is the total picture of nature that Prigogine and Stengers put forward, in which new relations or connections create, so to speak, new objects or select them from the possibilities that matter provides. The objects are not determined in advance, whereafter they interact within the boundaries of their once-and-for-all given properties, such as the mechanicists imagined it. On the contrary, one can say that the objects are selected or constituted as special objects for each other through their connections. It is not until after this that they interact within the boundaries of their connections.

Here, Prigogine and Stengers come close to Whitehead's "philosophy of *relation* - no element of nature is a permanent support for changing relations; each receives its identity from its relations with others - .... a philosophy of *innovating becoming*" (1984, p. 95, P & S's italics). They also talk of nature as active (p. 286).

Prigogine and Stengers accept that the so-called mechanical laws (i.e. those that are time-reversible) apply to some connections that objects can participate in, for example, as single particles in certain non-chemical interactions with low energy, and not to others such as ensembles. But they do not accept mechanicism, i.e. the mechanistic view of the world, and its belief that objects exist independently of, and before, their connections. This distinction, and with it the demarcation of the area of application of mechanical laws, has been, according to Prigogine and Stengers (1984, p. 252-53), an unsolved problem for classical dialectical materialism (e.g. in Engels' *Dialectics of nature*. See Engels, 1974).

7   Interim conclusions concerning the concept of activity

The main purpose of my above review was to demonstrate that the activity concept, defined by the so-called "three-stage schema of analysis" or "the postulate of indirectness", is already applied within the realm of inanimate nature. Here, as well as in psychology, one speaks of objects as only interacting within the boundaries of, or of being propagated or mediated by, a particular connection that can assume qualitatively different forms. The connection is also "active" in that it is not totally determined by its conditions, but also houses spontaneous features - so-called symmetry-breaking - that exceed the order or symmetry that existed in other dimensions of connections. This does not mean that inanimate nature is active in the same way as living subjects[10] are, but

---

[10]   It may be difficult to directly see in what way many everyday things, e.g. tables and chairs, are "active". The fundamental point of view here, however, is that matter, as such, is active, and that it is on this basis (like a figure on a ground) that it should be explained why matter, under certain circumstances, can display great stability. Niels Bohr (1958; 1964) also presented the problem in this way, and attempted to discover those properties in the eternally mov-

merely that the concept of activity, as such, is not sufficient in itself to define the specific characteristics of life or of the psyche - or of subjectivity. Reference to the principle of activity - to the "propagated" or "mediated" relationships and to the active connections, is then, merely a general philosophical means of dissociation from mechanism. This is both justifiable and necessary in a critique of mechanistic psychology. But it is not in itself sufficient as a means of pointing out or delimitting that which is uniquely subjective or psychic - and certainly not that which is uniquely human.

In completely the same way, it is not in itself wrong when Marx and Engels[11] say that

> "Men can be distinguished from animals by consciousness, by religion or anything else you like. They themselves begin to distinguish themselves from animals as soon as they begin to *produce* their means of subsistence ..... By producing their means of subsistence men are indirectly producing their material life." (Marx & Engels, 1976, p. 37).

Although it applies to more than just man, it is true enough that he, so to speak, produces, defines or abstracts himself through the act of entering into the essential connections in which he came into being and through which he develops. And our task in seeking a *scientific* knowledge of things is, quite rightly, to capture in *our* abstractions the *real* abstractions - the essential or active connections or relations. Marx and Engels formulate a *general* methodological principle and at the same time they apply it to man. But they have not as yet conceptually abstracted or defined man so as to distinguish him from animals. That requires a statement of the specific way in which man produces himself.

It is probably important to keep the more critical and general discussions of methodology apart from discussions that inside the framework of the former are more constructive and specific to a single science, as psychology, even though it may be difficult in the heat of the battle.

8   An illustrative model of activity as real abstraction

In section 5 of this paper I attempted to interpret the concept "activity" as abstraction or "real abstraction". Maybe some will feel that it is a poorly chosen term, especially if it is also to be applied to non-living nature.

I have considered other terms, but could not improve on "abstraction". One could perhaps say that the objects "create" each other and themselves in

---

ing micro-world that were necessary conditions for the macro-world's relative stability.

[11]   In *The German ideology*. See Marx & Engels, 1976, p. 37.

their relationships or connections, but that sounds too idealistic. One could also say that the objects "define" each other in their relationships, but I think that sounds too mentalistic. By saying "abstraction" I indicate precisely that the objects do not define or create each other out of nothing. On the contrary, they "extract" each other out of matter's infinite possibilities. Maybe my partiality for the concept of abstraction is also connected with a picture or model that I have used in various contexts as a metaphor[12].

This model, which we may call the "camel-model" is shown in its simplest form in figure 1:

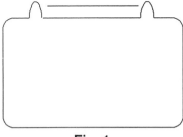

Fig. 1

The two "humps" are objects that are united in an activity, an active relationship or connection, indicated by the horizontal line. The lower continuous or "connected" piece is the objects' materiality, understood as the infinity of connections - the "context" - they engage in, in addition to that activity that defines them as objects for each other in a relationship.

One can also say that the activity, or the active relationship, abstracts the objects as figures on a common ground. The objects are separated out as objects by being connected in the activity. To a new kind of lawful connection there is a corresponding new kind of object. The connections and objects arise, so to speak, with and through each other.

There are many examples of this, as has been mentioned, in physics. Electric force and charged particles arise with and through each other; substance with and through thermodynamics, etc. I will not go further into this here.

Another example is of more interest to us here - the arrival of those special objects we call subjects, with and through the beginning of life-activity.

---

[12]   The same model has been adopted by Fog (1986).

Life-activity is a special active connection which can presumably be defined as a new type of asymmetrical entropy-relation. Niels Engelsted, with reference to Leontiev and others, has discussed this in detail in his writings (1985, p. 103; 1989).

"Above", so to speak, this life-activity, there now arises the special case of psychic activity and therewith another new type of objects in the world, namely, objects that are not merely subjects, but subjects with a psyche[13].

One might perhaps illustrate this with an elaborated version of the "camel-model" as in figure 2:

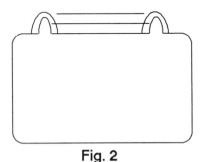

Fig. 2

Notice that at the same time as new subjects arrive, new objects also appear and vice versa[14]. Subjects that are equipped with a psyche are able to connect with, and make objects for their activity out of, other and much more comprehensive matters in the world, than subjects without a psyche (e.g. plants).

Figure 2 illustrates that there are simultaneously several qualitatively different "layers" in the individual's relationship to its surroundings, and that the "lower" layers are, so to speak, encased in the "higher" layers.

In section 10 I will return with examples to these qualitatively different layers in activity and therewith in the subjects and objects too.

The drawing in figure 2 is, of course, terribly primitive. That I dare present it anyway is due to the fact that it at least has some advantages over an al-

---

[13] Niels Engelsted, Leontiev and Henrik Poulsen disagree slightly about the nature of this new type of activity that abstracts subjects with a psyche. I name them here in alphabetical order, but this order also corresponds, I think, to the chronological stages in the development of the species at which each of them places the arrival of the psyche. See Niels Engelsted in this volume.

[14] The last mentioned implication, i.e. from the appearance of new objects for activity to the appearance of new subjects, is according to Leontiev, the dominating of the two in the development of the species and of the individual.

ternative that is more frequently seen. Two versions of this more traditional alternative are shown in figures 3 and 4.

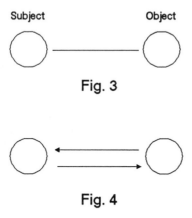

Subject   Object

Fig. 3

Fig. 4

In these figures it is very hard to see what distinguishes the relationship between subject and object from simple stimulation or interaction; one could perhaps call it an "external relation", or in Leontiev's words a "direct" or "two-stage" relation.

I have seen attempts in some schematic representations[15] to illustrate Leontiev's "postulate of indirectness" or the "three-stage schema of analysis" by drawing the activity as a particular instance between subject and object, as in figure 5.

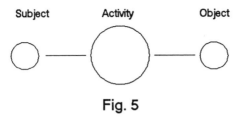

Subject   Activity   Object

Fig. 5

Such an illustration is, I believe, misleading. Firstly, because it tends to somewhat substantivise the activity concept; secondly, because it still resembles

---

[15] E.g. Hydén (1984, p. 116). Slightly different versions can be found in Schmidt, Thyssen and Hansen (1983, pp. 22, 24, 27), and Brostrøm (1983, p. 83).

normal mechanical interaction (merely with three stages); thirdly, because it does not indicate how the subject and object are abstracted by the activity; and finally, because it suggests that the connection between subject and object is, in one way or another, indirect, and actually becomes more and more indirect with the activity's growing complexity, whereas the opposite is nearer the truth. This last point is crucial. The development of activity brings us into closer and closer contact with still greater parts of, and still more layers of the world - it makes increasingly more of the world into objects for us.

The three-stage drawing is not far from being applicable as a good illustration of mechanicism's particular understanding of the relationship between subject and object, where a particular physical contact surface - a particular a priori communicative stage - is placed inbetween subject and object. I have expounded upon this more thoroughly in my book: *Den menneskelige sans* (The Human Sense) (1983).

It is for the above reasons that (as mentioned in section 4) I am not satisfied with Leontiev's terminology when he talks about a "three-stage schema of analysis" or "trinomial formula" and implicitly about the "postulate of indirectness".

As has been made apparent, I would prefer "the abstraction postulate", or maybe, if necessary, "the postulate of connectedness", or maybe even "the existence postulate". Subjects and objects "ex-ist", they "stand out from" matter by virtue of the connections through which they operate.

One of psychology's most important tasks now, as Leontiev (1978, pp. 141-143) himself formulates it, is to describe the concrete contents of the different levels in the activities that connect subject and object, and these levels' reciprocal relations or "transitions". What are the specific characteristics of life-activity as such?; of psychic activity as such?; of activity at different stages in life's development?. As an attempt to answer these questions Leontiev (1981) has outlined a taxonomy of human activities based on conceptual distinctions between the stages of irritability, sensation, perception, thought and consciousness (cf. section 10). At the same time this is also a taxonomy for the stages of phylogenetic development from the simplest forms of life to man, and a taxonomy for the comparative study of the activities of the different species living today.

Important questions for psychology are not just how all these connections are defined, but also how they are related in man, in whom they all play a role. In figure 6 the different levels in the human subject's connections to his surroundings are schematically represented in a further elaboration of the "camel-model".

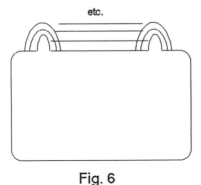

Fig. 6

It is not possible in the space available here to attempt to fully answer the above questions. Instead I present the outline of a basic understanding, within which an attempt at answering them can occur. In section 10, however, an attempt to answer a selected example from these questions will be intimated.

9 The "camel-model" as an explicit repudiation of reductionism (mechanicism, nominalism and epiphenomenalism)

The "camel-model" as outlined in figures 1, 2, and 6 is designed to illustrate an essential difference between a dialectical-materialistic and a reductionistic conception of the connections between subject and object.

The difference can maybe best be seen if we, as a contrast, imagine, as some reductionistic psychologists do, that the relationship between subject and object is like two computers communicating with each other.

Such an alternative mechanistic model which also distinguishes between different layers or levels of communication is shown in figure 7:

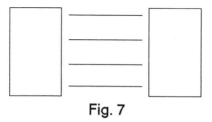

Fig. 7

At the bottom we have a physical process level where communication is described as electrical impulses. At the next level communication is described in a binary code (e.g. as 0's and 1's). Then there comes, for example, an alphanumerical level with letters and numbers, and finally, a word-level or symbolic level.

Depending upon our purpose, we can choose to conceive of the communication on one or another of these levels. For example, do we intend to monitor "the hardware", or do we wish to understand the machine's capacity to translate from Russian into English?

But regardless of these possible levels of conceptualisation, we have to admit that there does not occur any *real* interaction between the computers above the physical process level. A sufficiently detailed description at this level would be enough to explain the interaction.

In this sense the other levels of communication are, so to speak, *imaginary* - something we chose to ascribe to the interaction in order to make it easier to understand or use the processes involved.

We could then, for example, draw the higher "horizontal" lines between the computers in dotted form, as shown in figure 8, so as to indicate that they are "imaginary", derived constructions, and then in contrast to that, we could draw the real "vertical" connections between the levels within the computers as unbroken lines to indicate the real "translations" or the "coding processes" from level to level. Finally, the lowest "horizontal" line between the computers could also be drawn as unbroken to indicate the computers' real, physical interaction. Any dotted line can now be viewed merely as a convenient "short-cut" description of a process that in reality operates along the unbroken lines.

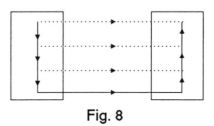

Fig. 8

In other words, the higher "horizontal" connections are in reality "epiphenomenal" or purely derived in relation to the real coding and interaction processes.

As long as we stick to computers we can all agree. But when this computer conception is used as an analogy or as a model for man's relationship to his surroundings it is no longer a statement of computers but of man. This is, in fact, the image of man embedded in modern mechanistic psychology that is supported when the computer analogy is used as a model, as it is, for example, in so-called "cognitive science" and in the application of artificial intelligence to psychology.

Also in these traditions one talks about different levels of description, corresponding to different purposes or interests (or "stances" as Dennett says). But only one of the levels is considered real, and houses the real interaction or contact between man and his surroundings. The other levels are imaginary, albeit useful ways of describing or designating the systems. The computer model of man's relations with his surroundings is, therefore, a modern version of nominalism.

I will not discuss this viewpoint in detail since I have done so elsewhere (see Mammen, 1983, 1985). I will merely state that an activity theory viewpoint, in contrast to this "nominalism" or "epiphenomenalism", would claim that the different levels of human activity are real and cannot be dissolved in each other; and that certainly makes a difference.

The actual desire to reduce the number of levels, exposed by the computer model, cannot in itself be critised. The attempt to avoid overcomplexity is a healthy scientific endeavour, and under certain circumstances it fortunately pays off. The method of breaking down or analysing complex relationships into simpler forms has, of course, been able to celebrate indisputable triumphs in the course of scientific history.

But if it can be convincingly argued that the different levels in this particular case cannot be reduced to each other, then it is unreasonable to work with a model that assumes that they can.

10 Psychological arguments for the "camel-model" and against reductionist interpretation of the subject-object relationship

The "camel-model" outlined above is just a skeleton that needs to be clothed in flesh and blood in order to become a psychological theory. To this end it is necessary that the different "levels" in the activities, the subjects and the objects are concretely designated.

For example, we might use Leontiev's (1981) distinction between the following five levels[16].

1. The level of irritability, in which the objects of activity are chemical substances or physical energy in the surroundings that are directly necessary for life.

---

[16] By using this example I am not saying that there are no more or less than five "levels" in the subject-object relationship. Neither is it my intention to say that a "lowest" level does exist in the relationship between subject and object, or for that matter between objects. These questions are for the time being too comprehensive to allow further treatment of them here.

2. The level of sensation, in which the objects are biologically neutral qualities in the surroundings and the objective connections of these with the
substances that are necessary for life.
3. The level of perception, in which the objects are whole objects in the surroundings.
4. The level of intellect, in which functional relationships between whole
objects are also objects of the subject's activity.

All these levels are, according to Leontiev, common to man and the highest
developed animals, i.e. the anthropoids.

In addition to these levels, there is one more which applies to man alone:

5. The level of consciousness. With the aid of Leontiev (1982) this level can
be characterised by the fact that the genesis of the surroundings' objects
are also the objects of the subject's activity, or, put another way, the subjects relate actively to the surroundings' "historical deep structure".

There ought, of course, to be an argument for how all these five levels are
qualitatively different from each other, and why they cannot be reduced to
each other, and how they manage anyway to grow out of each other and operate together within the single individual's total life. Whether Leontiev actually
carries out such an argumentation is, to me, an open question, and I will not
attempt it here either.

I will make do with suggesting how the last level of activity - the level of
consciousness - is separated qualitatively from the lower levels, and how it in
principle cannot be reduced to these[17].

The nucleus of my argument is that common to all the levels that are
lower than the level of consciousness, is the fact that the relation between
subject and object depends on what we may call universal qualities of the
subjects and objects. The subjects relate through their activity to, or abstract, a
sum of qualities in the object, including the object's quality of being reifiable.

The subjects are capable of learning and remembering, which means
that they can relate to objects in ways that depend on whether or not they have
had earlier experience with *similar* objects. The subjects can recognise the object's qualities and in a certain sense have an active "history".

As far as the most developed animals are concerned, it is also possible
that in a very few areas, e.g. in the relationship to their young, parents or mate,
they cannot only recognise these objects' qualities but also their so-called
"numerical identity" - their identity with themselves over time - regardless of

---

[17] I have previously argued more thoroughly for the claims I make here (e.g.
Mammen, 1983; 1985; 1986).

the qualities' constancy or variance within certain boundaries. There is in that case not only talk of recurrent recognition but of a more lasting attachment.

Regardless of whether the most developed animals can do this or not within their "spheres of intimacy", it is in any case clear that they are unable to manage such a lasting attachment or maintained connection to objects as such. Animals cannot abstract objects' continued existence in time, or make this into an object for themselves, beyond the single or repeated act of recognition. For example, even chimpanzees have no relationship to their tools (sticks etc.) beyond those situations in which they have needed them. Animals do not make objects in the world into "their" objects in the same way as man does.

Animals are similarly not capable of abstracting an object's genesis - of seeing it as a product with a history or as a cultural product.

On the other hand, man has this ability to unite himself with the objects in his surroundings in lasting connections, or a relationship of solidarity, and thus he transcends, as it were, the purely qualitative recognition of objects.

This ability is the foundation of the whole of man's identity formation, beginning with the relationship to one's parents and the family's "possessions" and ending with the relationship to human culture - its history and its products. For some implications of this view to applied psychology, see Fog (1986), Hem (1986), Bertelsen & Hem (1987, pp. 399-407), and Bertelsen (1988, pp. 25-29).

Concerning the question of the qualitative difference between the human level of consciousness and the levels that are lower in relation to this, it is interesting that from simple and plausible assumptions about the structural or "topological" relation between, on the one hand, objects' qualitative similarities and differences - so-called "qualitative identity", and on the other hand, objects' identity with themselves and difference to all others over time, regardless of qualitative changes - so-called "numerical identity", one can in effect argue logically and convincingly that the conscious relationship (as it is defined here) cannot be reduced to the relationships between subject and object on the lower levels.

And, what is even more important, is that the relations at the lower levels do not "converge" to the higher levels in an orderly, approximating way that is similar to the convergence of physics' simple, idealised models (e.g. the mathematical pendulum) to reality (e.g. real pendulums).

As a consequence of that, the theoretical models developed to describe the lower levels are not to be considered "approximations" to the essential and specific characteristics of man's connections with his world.

On the other hand there is a relation of correspondence between the levels that explains why it has been possible in the history of ideology, philosophy and psychology to find scientific arguments for a reductionist understanding of man.

The more detailed and elaborated argumentation, as I have presented it elsewhere[18], is relatively technical and makes use of concepts from mathematical logic and set theory. I believe that it is the first time - in psychology at least - that the chain of arguments against reductionism has been given that kind of formal exposition. A further gain with this formal procedure is the fact that not only the levels' qualitative differences, but also their mutual dependence and attachment is described. By borrowing the language of mathematics and physics, one can say that the relation between the various levels is not only characterised by "transcendence", but also by "correspondence"[19].

11   References

Bertelsen, P. (1988). Kategorier, modeller og metaforer i kulturpsykologi. (Categories, models, and metaphors in cultural psychology). *Psyke & Logos, 9*(1), 23-59.

Bertelsen, P. & Hem, L. (1987). Om begrebet: Klientens model af verden. (On the concept: The client's model of the world). *Psyke & Logos, 8*(2), 375-408.

Bohr, N. (1958). *Atomic physics and human knowledge, Lectures 1932-1957,* New York: John Wiley.

Bohr, N. (1964). *Essays 1958-1962 on atomic physics and human knowledge.* New York: John Wiley.

Brostrøm, S. (1983). *Virksomhed og personlighedsudvikling.* (Activity and the development of personality). Copenhagen: Børn og Unge.

Dreier, O. (1974). En præsentation og vurdering af Leontjevs almene psykologi. (A presentation and evaluation of Leontiev's general psychology). *Udkast, 2*(2), 247-351.

Dreier, O. (1981). Psykologien som en historisk-materialistisk videnskab. Om A.N. Leontjevs almene psykologi. (Psychology as an historical-materialistic science - A.N. Leontiev's general psychology). *Psyke & Logos, 2*(1), 7-49.

Dreier, O. (1983). A.N. Leontjev: Virksomhed og personlighed. (A.N. Leontiev: Activity and personality). *Nordisk Psykologi, 35*(4), 272-295.

Engels, F. (1974). *Dialectics of nature.* Moscow: Progress Publishers.

---

[18]   The argument is presented in my book *Den menneskelige sans* (The Human Sense) (Mammen, 1983), and can be viewed as a critical development of Strawson's logical argumentation in *Individuals* (Strawson, 1964).

[19]   I believe it is something along these lines that Leontiev is searching for at the end of his book *Activity, Consciousness, and Personality* (1978, pp. 141-143), where he sets up the further perspective for psychology to study – that which he calls the "transfers" or "transitions" (transformations) between the qualitatively different levels of activity.

Engelsted, N. (1984). *Springet fra dyr til menneske.* (The leap from animal to man). Copenhagen: Dansk psykologisk Forlag.

Engelsted, N. (1985). *Om den politiske natur: En analyse af forholdet mellem biologi og psykologi.* (Political nature: An analysis of the relationship between biology and psychology). Institute of Psychology, Aarhus University. (Earlier edition: Copenhagen: Antropos, 1981).

Engelsted, N. (1989). *Personlighedens almene grundlag I og II.* (The general foundation of personality, volumes I and II). Århus: Aarhus University Press.

Fog, J. (1986). Adskilt i forbundethed. (Separated in unity). *Psyke & Logos,* 7(1), 86-108.

Hawking, S. (1988). Hvorfor går tiden ikke baglæns? (Why does time not go backwards?). *Forskning & Samfund, 14,* no. 3, 16-22.

Hem, L. (1986). Nornerne spinder. Noter til Mammens artikel. (The Norns are spinning. Notes on Mammen's article). *Psyke & Logos,* 7(1) 203-204.

Hydén, L.C. (1984). *Psykologi og materialisme.* (Psychology and materialism). Copenhagen: Munksgaard. (Swedish edition, 1981).

Karpatschof, B. (1984). Følelsernes fylogenese. (The phylogenesis of emotions). *Psyke & Logos,* 5(1), 32-53.

Lenin, V.I. (1972). Materialism and empirio-criticism. Critical comments on a reactionary philosophy. In: V.I. Lenin: *Collected works, Vol. 14.* Moscow: Progress Publishers. (Russian edition 1909).

Leontiev, A.N. (1978). *Activity, consciousness, and personality.* Englewood Cliffs, N.J.: Prentice-Hall. (Russian edition, 1977).

Leontiev, A.N. (1981). *Problems of the development of the mind.* Moscow: Progress Publishers. (Russian edition, 1959).

Leontiev, A.N. (1982). Psychologie des Abbilds. (Psychology of the perceptual image). *Forum kritische Psychologie, 9,* 5-9. (Translated from a Russian manuscript, 1975).

Lewin, K. (1931). The conflict between Aristotelian and Galilean modes of thought in contemporary psychology. *Journal of General Psychology, 5,* 141-177. (Reprinted in: Lewin, K.: *A dynamic theory of personality.* New York: McGraw-Hill, 1935, pp. 1-42).

Mammen, J. (1983). *Den menneskelige sans. Et essay om psykologiens genstandsområde.* (The human sense. An essay on psychology's subject matter). Copenhagen: Dansk psykologisk Forlag.

Mammen, J. (1985). Menneskets bevidsthed. (Human consciousness). In: O. Fenger & S. Jørgensen (eds.): *Skabelse, udvikling, samfund. En forelæsningsrække. Acta Jutlandica LX, samfundsvidenskabelig serie 16.* Århus: Arkona, pp. 73-81 and 271.

Mammen, J. (1986). Erkendelsen som objektrelation. (Knowing as object-relation). *Psyke & Logos,* 7(1), 178-202.

Marx, K. (1973). *Grundrisse, foundations of the critique of political economy,* London: Pelican (Originally 1857. Translated from Marx/Engels: *Werke, Bd. 13.* Berlin (DDR): Dietz Verlag).

Marx, K. & Engels, F. (1976). *The German ideology*. Moscow: Progress Publishers (Originally 1846. Translated from Marx/Engels: *Werke Bd. 3.* Berlin (DDR): Dietz Verlag).

Nørretranders, T. (1985). *Det udelelige. Niels Bohrs aktualitet i fysik, mystik og politik.* (The indivisible. Niels Bohr's topicality in physics, mysticism and politics). Copenhagen: Gyldendal.

Poulsen, H. (1982). Leontjev, genspejlingsbegrebet og den almene psykologi. (Leontiev, the concept of reflectivity and general psychology). *Psyke & Logos, 3*(1) 161-175.

Poulsen, H. (1985). Om redskabskonstruktion og menneskelig psyke. (On the construction of tools and the human psyche). In O. Fenger & S. Jørgensen (eds.): *Skabelse, udvikling, samfund. En forelæsningsrække. Acta Jutlandica LX, samfundsvidenskabelig serie 16.* Århus: Arkona, pp. 49-55 and 270.

Prigogine, I. & Stengers, I. (1984). *Order out of chaos. Man's new dialogue with nature.* New York: Bantam Books.

Rubinstein, S.L. (1973). *Sein und Bewusstsein.* (Being and consciousness). Berlin: Akademie Verlag. (Russian edition, 1957).

Schmidt, Aa., Thyssen, S. & Hansen, V.R. (1983): *Virksomhed, udvikling og undervisning.* (Activity, development, and teaching). Copenhagen: Forlaget Tiden. (Marxistisk pædagogik og psykologi 8).

Schultz, E. (1988). *Personlighedspsykologi på erkendelsesteoretisk grundlag - eller mysteriet om personen der forsvandt.* (A psychology of personality from the perspective of the theory of knowledge - or the mystery of the person who vanished). Copenhagen: Dansk psykologisk Forlag.

Strawson, P.F. (1964). *Individuals.* London: Methuen (University Paperbacks). (Original, 1959).

The Concept of Observation in Physics and Psychology[1]

I.K. Moustgaard

The classic concept of observation

According to more recent studies in the history of science the general scientific concept of observation appears to have developed from the classical observational situation in astronomy.

A.J. Sabra's (1971) analysis seems to show that the brilliant Arabic researcher Ibn-al-Haitham (965-1039) did not as yet have the concept of experiment (Latin: experimentum) at his disposal. Rather, the word he used in his texts for scientific observation was *ictibar* which means attempting through direct observation to determine the connection between chosen variables.

It was not before much later that there arose the idea of being able to observe while at the same time having full control over relevant variables - including variables related to the observer. I will not chart the earlier history of the concept of experimentation here. I merely wish to point out that there appear to be various early sources of the concept of observation - that concept which is so closely related within psychology to experimentation and the prolonged efforts to neutralise, so to speak, the observer's influence upon that which is observed and hence upon results.

Let us consider yet another episode in the history and development of the concept of observation: Kant's widely discussed ideas in "Metaphysische Anfangsgründe der Naturwissenschaften" (Kant, 1839). Here it is said that "selbst die Beobachtung an sich schon den Zustand des beobachteten Gegenstandes alteriert und verstellt" (even the observation by itself disturbs and distorts the state of the observed object) (Kant, 1839, p. 310) .

Despite what one might think, however, psychology was not the target of this comment, but rather *chemistry*, with which we today have no problem in placing under the *natural* sciences.

Of psychological observation it was said: "Sie kann (daher) niemals etwas mehr als eine historische, und, als solche, so viel möglich systematische Naturlehre des inneren Sinnes das ist eine Naturbeschreibung der Seele, aber nicht Seelenwissenschaft, ja nicht einmal psychologische Experimentallehre werden" (It can never be more than a historical, and as such as systematic as

---

[1] Part of this article follows an earlier version by Moustgaard (1986).

possible, natural philosophy of inner sense, i.e. a natural description of the soul. But it cannot become a science of the soul, not even a psychological, experimental science) (p. 311).

Here the *ideal* form of observation is clearly stated: The only form of observation which is scientifically acceptable is that which is able in principle to live up to the classic demand concerning the observation of something *external* to the observer, which is that the actual act of observation must not in itself have an effect on that which is observed and thereby influence the data resulting from the observation.

But this, of course, *only* concerns an ideal. There were many well known practical and scientific situations which broke this principle, and these have become more common in the years since. However, Kant would probably never have considered it possible that in the following 100 years even physics would have to, in principle, abandon the absolute ideal concerning neutral observation.

Niels Bohr

It is well known that Niels Bohr was not only interested in the observational problems in physics but also in the development of psychology's concept of observation. In the following pages my main concern will be to give an account of and discuss Bohr's view on psychology's concept of observation. For instance, his attempt throughout the whole of his active life to determine the differences, or maybe rather the similarities, between observation in psychology and observation in quantum physics.

Strange as it may sound, the following account should not be primarily considered as historical. Its relevance in the present context is that it gives occasion for rummaging through all the central problems concerning scientific (controllable) observation.

Bohr's thoughts on observation in physics and psychology

Despite Bohr's frequent and clear emphasising that his views on complementarity "were far from containing anything at all against the spirit of science fighting mysticism" (Bohr, 1957, p. 39), he has often been misunderstood on precisely this point. The fact that he has often used examples concerning human feelings and volition that have been difficult to understand, when he wished to "find genuine parallels with the information derived from atomic theory concerning the limited validity of idealisations" (p. 30), has contributed to this.

The problem of observation within psychology is in the eyes of many so unclarified that one would rather concern oneself with psychology's dwindling possibilities of living up to science's demand for objective description than with the many cases in which this demand is easily fulfilled. Therefore, my efforts in what is to come will be concerned, firstly, with documenting that Bohr's views on complementarity in atomic physics do *not*, according to his own opinion, involve a deviation from the classic demand to every science that the observing researcher must be able to be seen as standing outside of that that is being observed, and secondly, with demonstrating that the science of psychology, despite its obvious difficulties in this connection, is similarly capable of achieving objective observation and description.

In my opinion Bohr expresses his views concerning this classic demand in physics most clearly in "Atomerne og den menneskelige erkendelse" (Atoms and Human Knowledge) (1955). It is stated here: "We must, of course, maintain in every area of experience a sharp distinction between the observer and the contents of the observed, but we must bear in mind that the discovery of quantum effects has placed even the foundations of our *description* of nature in a new light, and taught us about hitherto unnoticed premises concerning the rational application of those concepts upon which the communication of the experiences rests" (pp. 109 - 110), (italics mine).

Bohr goes on to discuss the definition of the phenomena in question: "In quantum physics .... an account of the functions of measuring instruments is absolutely necessary for defining phenomena, and we must draw the line, so to speak, between the subject and the object in a way that ensures in every single case the unambiguous application of the elementary physical concepts used in the communication", (Bohr, 1957).

So much then for the possibilities of nuclear physics to live up to the demand for objective observation and description. But what about psychology's possibilities in this respect?

We will look more closely at this question in the following considerations which attempt to examine the possibilities within psychology of distinguishing sharply between subject and object.

Objective observation in psychology

Bohr points out that psychologists had clearly recognised their science's problems of observation long before corresponding problems became important within the natural sciences (Bohr, 1957, p. 33). An example of this can be seen in his contribution to the festschrift published in honour of Max Planck's 50th year as a doctor of philosophy in 1929, where Bohr deals with a problem that has occupied philosophers and psychologists throughout a long period in the history of ideas. According to Bohr's elaboration the problem consists in the fact that the observation and description of our own "thought activity" requires "on the one hand, that objectively given thought content be studied by a subject", while on the other hand, "a sharp distinction between object and subject cannot be maintained since the concept of a subject belongs to or is part of our thought activity" (1929a, p. 484).

This complicated question may be formulated slightly differently so as to express the following question concerning our concept of consciousness: Can the actively observing part of our consciousness, as well as observing objects that are foreign to itself, also turn itself and its knowledge processes into an object of observation and description?

Bohr is naturally correct in suggesting that our everyday experiences show us that this actively observing part of consciousness (call it the subject, the self, attention, or whatever name one prefers) *can* be turned into the object of our own observation and description, and thus may present itself as an observed phenomenon amongst other such phenomena.

However, closer consideration shows that a precondition is necessary for the above assumption, i.e. that a new I so to speak manifests itself in the consciousness of the person. Acknowledgement of this consequence appears to start one off on the feared endless spiral where new I's are the forced consequence of each previously acknowledged I.

Bohr was also amused by this consequence, as can be seen for example in his lecture: "The unity of human knowledge" held during the European Cultural Fund's Congress in Copenhagen in October 1960 (Bohr, 1964). He quotes the passage from Poul Martin Møller's "En dansk students eventyr" (A Danish Student's Adventures) where "the two cousins (the philistine and the licentiate) keenly discuss the problems they have had during their lives. Upon being reproached for not having achieved anything practical in his life the licentiate excuses himself with the following argument:

> "My endless studying and searching means that I achieve nothing. Furthermore, I come to think about my own thoughts, and on top of that I think about the fact that I am thinking. I divide myself up into an infinitely regressing series of I's that contemplate each other. I do not know which I eventually remains as the real one when I stop, and in that moment when I do stop with a particular I, there is always another I waiting. I become confused and dizzy as if I was staring down into an abyss, and these contemplations end with my getting an awful headache"." (Bohr, 1964, p. 24-25).

I ought here to use this quote as a reason for thoroughly analysing the necessary features of an adequate concept of consciousness, but such an undertaking would require too much time and space and prevent me from continuing to allow Bohr's thoughts to guide this discussion.

Bohr again takes up the theme from Planck's festschrift 30 years later during the opening lecture of the above named congress ("The Unity of Human Knowledge"). There can hardly be any doubt, however, that his opinion changes somewhat in the meantime. It is clear that in his earlier work Bohr was more pessimistic about the problem of description concerning how consciousness relates to itself. Thus, in 1929 he stresses that in many cases it is *impossible* to maintain an *absolute* distinction between object and subject in psychology. In the opening lecture from 1960 he merely strongly advises psychological researchers to be very thorough in specifying the necessary *borderline* between object and subject during the course of observation.

Furthermore, Bohr correctly states that we are only led into an infinite regress because we "search for a final subject", but such an endeavour "is contrary to the nature of objective description which requires that the subject and object are placed in contrast with each other", (Bohr, 1964, p. 26). We will later return to this line of thought.

The boundary between subject and object

Thus, despite the theoretical problems involved, Bohr maintains the need for a well defined boundary between object and subject - between the described and the describer - also in the case of psychology's scientific observations. This can, for example, also be seen in the following words: "Every unambiguous statement concerning our state of mind implies, *of course*, a distinction between the contents of our consciousness and the background which we casually refer to as "ourselves". But every attempt to fully describe the wealth of mental life requires that in the varying situations the line of division between subject and object is placed differently". (Bohr, 1964, p. 24) (italics mine).

This relentless and often heavily stressed demand for a precise distinction between subject and object in all cases of scientific description, including psychology, has as its consequence the acceptance of two necessary aspects of our conscious life which have been referred to as consciousness' *intentionality* and *reflectivity*.

In Denmark these two main features of conscious activity have been given thorough consideration from a theory of knowledge perspective by Knud Grue-Sørensen (1950) in his doctoral dissertation: "Studier over refleksivitet" (Studies in Reflectivity). Referring the reader to this work frees me from having to discuss this problem more closely. I will therefore limit the discussion here to a few remarks.

Grue-Sørensen characterises intentionality as that condition in which conscious activity is directed towards something other than itself. Conscious activity is said to *always* be in this condition - it is, put briefly, always object directed. On the other hand, reflectivity describes how consciousness' active observation can also be directed towards the processes of consciousness.

There is a clear contradiction in this formulation. If consciousness is always in a condition of intentionality then it would not appear possible that it could also "reflect upon itself" as it has been expressed.

Bohr has in several connections stressed the importance of the concept of consciousness (which I will return to), and he shows in his examples that he believes it to involve both intentionality and reflectivity. However, in his earlier formulations he is rather ambiguous with respect to the status of these characteristics of consciousness. Thus, he claims that it is not necessary to consider them both as fundamental facts if we wish to avoid the type of tricky problems within the theory of knowledge that Poul Møller poked fun at.

It goes without saying that a comprehensive description of consciousness in concrete situations does *not* imply an account of an unending sequence of so-called "regressing" I's and their conscious processes. Anyone who considers his own experience will be convinced of this, and it was, of course, also obvious to Møller (cf. Moustgaard, 1964).

Many will certainly grant that one sometimes, in the words of the licentiate, thinks about one's own thoughts, e.g. in order to control the quality of one's thoughts when trying to solve problems. But the above discussed regression is rarely experienced beyond this first step. In the Planck-festschrift Bohr calls attention to a circumstance that is crucial with respect to our understanding of the modest role played by reflectivity in everyday life. He points out that a conscious analysis of any thought situation and the direct application of the concept of reflectivity are mutually exclusive.

Moreover, this point which Bohr views as a clear example of the necessity of a so-called "reciprocal method of description" (this was his earlier name for complementarity), is in harmony with the distinction made by Harald Høffding (1910) in the beginning of "Den menneskelige Tanke. Dens former og dens opgaver" (The human thought: Its forms and tasks). Here a distinction is made between, on the one hand, "the involuntary or automatic life of the soul .... which expands previous to any mental reflection or afterthought", and on the other hand "the world of mental reflection". Høffding also considers these two forms of conscious functioning to be mutually exclusive: We cannot be simultaneously engaged in both worlds (cf. the so-called "Høffding's paradox"). Later I will return to this theme in connection with an analysis of Bohr's concept of attention.

It is certainly understandable that Bohr originally preferred to take his examples of psychological observation and description from the observation of so-called "internal" and "private" phenomena (cf. Jørgensen, 1955), for in the course of time they have, of course, been stumbling-blocks for many who have considered psychology's possibilities of objective observation, and have often prevented recognition of the fact that we, in principle, are faced with the same problems of description when we perceive and characterise "external" and "public" phenomena. It is a necessary condition of any observation, including the observation of public phenomena, that the phenomenon in question is available - or can become available - for observation. It is, of course, easiest to acknowledge this general condition when we, for example, select the perception and experience of the immediate phenomena of everyday life while advanced sciences such as physics usually work with the indirect registering of phenomena via inserted observational mediums and control procedures (cf. pointer-readings).

No matter how important this difference is with respect to issues of methodology and control, it does not have any fundamental significance in connection with our current analysis of the situation of observation in psychology.

It appears from my sources that Bohr employed the concept of "self-observation" in many connections without seeing any problems in this use of language. He appears to have taken over the concept from earlier Danish psychologists without closer, critical consideration and without seeking a more exact definition. Judging by the contexts in which it is used what is meant is the person's observation of his own phenomena, but this apparently only includes "inner" and "private" phenomena.

Even though one could presume it from the name "self-observation" it is not used to specify the person's own observation of his own *self*-phenomena - "inner" as well as "external", private as well as "public".

The observational situation where the observing person concentrated upon his "own" phenomena was by far the most prevalent in older psychology. Niels Bohr's philosophy and psychology teacher at University - the above named Harald Høffding, represented the widespread opinion that ascribes to "self-observation" or the person's observation of his own phenomena an almost absolute significance in empirical psychology. This view came later to be somewhat disparagingly called "writing-table psychology" (cf. Høffding, 1882).

Two principle forms of observation in psychology

In order to provide a more ordered picture I will survey psychology's observational situations from the perspective of the two following distinct forms which are different in principle.

Firstly, the just discussed situation where the psychological researcher concerns himself with his own phenomenological world in various conditions with a view to describing it as well as he can and communicating the results of his observations to colleagues and other interested parties. I will call this observational situation E (for ego).

Secondly, the equally important situation where the researcher observes another person's reactions and through these attempts to gain access to the subject's phenomenological world. Among the person's reactions an important type is naturally the communication of meaning and opinion that must necessarily occur between the researcher and the experimental subject in the observational situation (cf. Moustgaard, 1987). I will call this observational situation A (for alter).

As mentioned above, Bohr originally had a special interest in situation E and especially in the observation of "internal" and "private" phenomena (i.e. introspection). In such cases it is often *im*possible to distinguish completely between the poles of object and subject during observation. In those instances where it has to be acknowledged that such a distinction cannot be made, one ought to describe one's results as aesthetic, literary, or something similar, rather than as pertaining to scientific psychology. This does not in the slightest devalue such data.

The possibilities of also undertaking an objective observation of "internal" and "private" phenomena are heavily dependent upon such conditions as the existence of an adequate conceptual apparatus, the experience of the researcher in introspection, etc. Therefore, one cannot generally and once and forever consider such phenomena as inaccessible to objective observation.

To give a concrete example, one could reflect upon the problems connected with the description of the phenomena of pain. Such observation and description still plays a role in practical medicine.

This concurs with the view of Bohr expressed in the quotation above, namely, that concrete attempts to describe the wealth of conscious mental life requires a different positioning of the dividing line between subject and object in the various observational situations (Bohr, 1964, p. 24).

The feature of Niels Bohr's analysis that most convincingly reveals his view, and which is of crucial importance to an understanding of the psychological concept of observation, is that he does not tend to fall into the conventional, but misleading, interpretation of the classic demand concerning the position of the observer as being *outside* of that that is being observed. He does not interpret this demand in purely spatial terms, and thus avoids the paradoxes that such an interpretation inevitably involves.

The most serious mistake of traditional behaviourism was that it regarded the only way to be objective was by literally placing the observer outside of that to be observed. In this way psychology became in the words of the

Norwegian psychologist K.H. Teigen, a science which is only concerned with "the others", and not with the researcher himself (Teigen, 1981; 1983).

Here though, one overlooks the fact that an adequate interpretation of other's behaviour (including, of course, their communicative behaviour) is dependent on the researcher's own conscious involvement in the observational situation (Moustgaard, 1987). We will return to this argument later.

As mentioned, Bohr did not subscribe to this widespread misunderstanding of the fundamental conditions of description. In the previously mentioned lecture on the unity of knowledge he specifies his view on the relevance of other people's behaviour (their "conduct") to our psychological understanding of them as persons in the following words:

> As far as our knowledge of other living creatures is concerned, we are, of course, only witnesses to their conduct, but one has to understand that the word consciousness is unavoidable when such conduct is so complicated that its description, in our common language, results in a reference to the self-knowledge of the party in question. (Bohr, 1964, p. 26).

In his later work, Bohr becomes more and more optimistic with respect to the possibilities of psychology living up to the requirement for independence between the object of observation and description and the actively observing and describing person.

This independence can, of course, be ensured by the effective endeavour to follow a well defined borderline during the course of description. In Bohr's own words:

> If our endeavours to give an account of our mental state meet with difficulties regarding our ability to remain as outside observers, it is still possible, to a great extent, to satisfy the demand for objective description even in human psychology. (Bohr, 1957, p. 93-94)[2]

Bohr's concept of attention

I will now briefly mention Bohr's problems with the concept of attention.

It has been normal for centuries to label, as Bohr does, that active element of consciousness that is held responsible for observation and description as *attention*. There would, of course, thus far, be nothing to object to, if it was not for the fact that this concept is used like a kind of apparatus inside consciousness to explain the self-same processes that attention actually consists of.

---

[2]   These words are from the lecture *The Unity of Knowledge*, given in October, 1954 at Columbia University, U.S.A.

This is then a case of explanatory circularity (cf. more recent cognitive psychology).

There can hardly be any doubt though, that this widespread tendency to misuse the concept of attention has been strengthened by the fact that modern Danish no longer includes the verb "at opmærke" (to attend), which was still in general use in the 18th century to describe the activity of concentrating upon something. (We now, of course, only have the noun "opmærksomhed" (attention)).

As has been said, Bohr uses in several connections the concept of "attention" without mentioning its weaknesses. In the treatise "Light and Life"[3], Bohr talks about the long known problem of description in psychology concerning the fact that concentrated attention appears to have a distorting effect upon the phenomenal world of the describing person. Bohr brings up this subject because he sees in this a "true analogy" to conditions in micro-physics. Bohr states:

> The necessity of taking into consideration the interaction between measuring instruments and the objects of investigation in nuclear physics, corresponds closely to the singular difficulties that we meet in psychological analyses that stem from the fact that the contents of consciousness invariably change when attention is engaged in some distinct feature. (Bohr, 1957, p. 20).

Judging by this it would seem that Bohr is of the opinion that prior to such a "psychological analysis" the contents of consciousness exist in a clear and, so to speak, untouched form. Attention is then directed at an individual feature of consciousness. This feature becomes accentuated at the expense of other features and this effect leads "invariably", as he says, to a change, or even a distortion, of the original thought content.

The analogy with nuclear physics then consists in attention's selecting function's correspondence to the operation of measuring instruments, while the original (untouched) thought content corresponds to the object of investigation.

However, Bohr had already and justifiably specified that the fundamental instruction that, in his opinion, we have obtained from quantum mechanics does not concern basic problems of measurement and registration, but, in the words of Bohr:

---

[3] This was originally the manuscript of a lecture held at the opening meeting of the second international congress for light therapy in Copenhagen in 1932.

.... the fundamental limitation of our customary conception of the phenomena as existing independently of the means by which they are observed (ibid. p. 16).

In the treatise "Discussion with Einstein on Theory of Knowledge Problems in Nuclear Physics", which was finished in 1949 and published in 1957, Bohr again emphasises this view, aiming his remarks at those who have interpreted him in terms such as *the disturbance of phenomena through observation*.

Moreover, he recommends for the sake of clarity that one reserve the term "phenomenon" for those situations where the observational data are obtained under given and specified circumstances, including a detailed report of experimental procedures (ibid. p. 79). Such a tightening of the use of language would undoubtedly also have a reorganising influence on empirical psychology. All in all, there can hardly be any doubt that Bohr's misleading concept of attention has caused him to come into conflict with his own basic view.

If one is to talk of a more thorough analogy between attention's mode of operation and the state of quantum mechanics, one must abandon all ideas of thought content untouched by the workings of consciousness.

Man is certainly capable of imagining himself facing his phenomena in their immediate and "untouched" form, but we cannot, in principle, realise this situation, for as soon as we - metaphorically speaking - try to reach out after these phenomena in order to freeze them in description, they must necessarily be characterised in one or another conceptual form that can serve us during further analysis, or form part of the communication of the results of our observation to our fellow man.

Psychology has no more hope than quantum physics of identifying phenomena independently of the methods that are necessary for their observation.

The basis for Bohr's view concerning the influence of attention is apparently the experience, that is familiar to us all, of sometimes not being able to transfer to terminologically safe ground, without damage, the structures of insight that one feels intensely in possession of when one attempts to articulate this insight. There is, however, no basis for generalising such situations and their characteristic features to "psychological analyses" in general.

The personal observer

During the talk held in connection with his reception of the Sonning prize in 1961 Bohr again discusses the condition which I touched upon earlier under the name of the necessary reflectivity of consciousness. After having mentioned that there is a long tradition in psychology for using basic concepts such as "thoughts" and "feelings" in a complementary fashion, Bohr continues thus:

In connection with this one must not forget that objective description of atomic phenomena touches precisely upon the detailed specification of the mutually exclusive experimental conditions, under which the complementary experiences are gained and reference to the personal observer is, therefore, not necessary. (Bohr, 1961).

To this one must ask: What is the position now with regard to psychology, does one have to refer to "the personal observer" with the consequences this would have for the possibility of achieving objective description? In Bohr's opinion the answer is *no*. In the treatise "Light and Life Revisited" from 1962 (which reconsiders the themes of the earlier mentioned introductory lecture), Bohr states:

While in objective physical description we naturally do not refer to the observing subject, when we talk about conscious experiences we do say "I think" or "I feel". The analogy with the requirement in quantum physics to consider all the essential features of the experimental arrangements, however, is reflected by the different verbs we connect with the pronouns". (Bohr, 1964, p. 42).

Bohr then goes on to once again jest with the old problem of the multiple I's who contemplate each other and dispute with each other - a problem that, as has been mentioned, one is forced into if one attempts, in the same way as Poul Møller's licentiate, to hunt down a *final* subject in the sequence of I's. About this Bohr continues:

While all search for a final subject is, of course, at variance with the essence of objective description which requires a contrast between the subject and object, the chances of preserving the unity of personality in man and of maintaining the notion of free will are qualified by the different placings of the dividing line between subject and object in situations that we label with words such as contemplation or instinctual urge. (Bohr, 1961).

There can hardly be any doubt in the mind of the careful reader that Bohr, in his later work, ascribes to psychology greater and more comprehensive possibilities of attaining objective descriptions. As far as I can see, this is due to a clearer recognition of the necessity of regarding the reflective nature of consciousness - its self-reference - as a fundamental fact that is co-ordinated with the object-orientation or intentionality of consciousness. Even the examples that were previously used to illustrate the *im*possibility of placing an absolute dividing section between the objective and subjective poles of the descriptive process, are now used to demonstrate the possibilities of an objective psychology.

For example, this can be seen in the following words from the lecture "Physics and the Problem of Life" which was one of the Steno lectures held in 1949, but the manuscript of which was not completed before 1957 (Bohr, 1957, p. 123):

> Compared with the expansion of mechanistic description which the reporting of the general features of atomic phenomena has required, the organism's integrity and unity of personality confront us with a much more far-reaching extension of the parameters of the rational usage of our means of communication.

He continues:

> In this respect it must be stressed that the distinction between subject and object which is necessary for unambiguous description is upheld if, when making any report that includes a reference to ourselves, we insert - so to speak - a new subject that is not part of the report's content.

This line of thought ends with the following optimistic words;

> It hardly needs to be underlined that it is precisely this freedom in the choice of the dividing line between subject and object that allows room for the multiplicity of the phenomena of consciousness and the possibilities of human life.

The communication of the results of observation

From Bohr's later work one can also see another important development. This involves his lessening interest in the form of observation that I called observational situation E, and an increasing interest in the other main form of observation - observational situation A and the related necessary communication between the researcher and the observing experimental subject.

Situation A must, of course, be seen as a complicated interaction between the two persons' observations, namely, the researcher's observation of the experimental subject's responses in connection with the latters observation of "external" and "internal" phenomena.

Here, Bohr naturally realises that the communication between the two persons in the experimental dyad is a necessity, and moreover, he emphasises that this communication of data must be viewed as a communication between two *equal partners*, that is to say, a communication that cannot be reduced to one party's observation of the other party's "external" behaviour.

As mentioned earlier, Bohr expresses his view, in part, by stressing the necessity of the concept of consciousness in psychology. This is aimed at a behaviouristic physicalism in the following words:

> ....when our concern is with human existence the use of the word consciousness is unavoidable, not only with reference to oneself, but also with reference to one's fellow man.

This is a quote from the lecture "The Unity of Knowledge" (Oct. 1954) (Bohr, 1957, p. 93). The same line of thought was also expressed during the previously mentioned talk in connection with Bohr's reception of the Sonning prize (Bohr, 1961).

In this connection Bohr also emphasises that a crucial condition for the clear and, in Bohr's term, "unambiguous" communication between the researcher and the experimental subject during their discussion, is the successful identification and specification of the actual dividing line between subject and object, from which the experimental subject carries out his observations and description, and the researcher his observation, description and control of data.

As is known, this requires of scientific psychology the systematic control of intersubject thought communication. This is a crucial control option in empirical research.

It is not possible to discuss more closely here these necessary forms of control. It can, however, be established that this intersubjective control of data communication requires that the researcher, so to speak, uses himself - his own perceptions of the observed objects as an instrument in deciding the extent to which descriptive concurrence exists between the partners in the observational situation.

This fact is the strongest argument against a one-sided behaviouristic interpretation of that observational situation which I have called situation A.

References

Bohr, N. (1929, a). Wirkungsquantum und Naturbeschreibung (The quantum of action and description of nature). *Die Naturwissenschaften, Heft 26.*

Bohr, N. (1929, b). Atomteori og Naturbeskrivelse (Atomic theory and description of nature), *Festskrift University of Copenhagen.*

Bohr, N. (1957). *Atomfysik og menneskelig Erkendelse, I* (Atomic physics and human knowledge, I). Copenhagen: Schultz, 1957.

Bohr, N. (1958). *Atomteori og Naturbeskrivelse* (Atomic theory and description of nature), Copenhagen: Schultz.

Bohr, N. (1961). *Atomvidenskaben og menneskehedens krise* (Atomic science and the crisis of humanity). Politikens kronik, 20.4.

Bohr, N. (1964). *Atomfysik og menneskelig erkendelse, II* (Atomic physics and human knowledge, II). Copenhagen: Schultz.

Grue-Sørensen, K. (1950). *Studier over Refleksivitet* (Studies in reflectivity). Copenhagen: Schultz.

Høffding, H. (1882). *Psykologi i omrids paa grundlag af erfaring* (An outline of psychology on an empirical basis). Copenhagen: Gyldendal.

Høffding, H. (1910). *Den menneskelige tanke. Dens former og dens opgaver* (The human thought. Its forms and its tasks). Copenhagen: Gyldendal.

Jørgensen, J. (1955). Hvad er psykology? Revideret udgave af kapitel VI. In: *Psykologi på biologisk grundlag*. Copenhagen: Munksgaard.

Kant, I. (1839). *Metaphysische Anfangsgründe der Naturwissenschaften* (Metaphysical foundations of the natural sciences). Berlin: Königliche Preussische Akademie der Wissenschaften.

Moustgaard, I.K. (1964). Om dækkende beskrivelser i perceptionspsykologien (On accurate descriptions in the psychology of perception). *Nordisk Psykologi, 16*, 287-304.

Moustgaard, I.K. (1986). Niels Bohr's tanker om psykologiens observationsbegreb (Niels Bohr's throughts on the concept of observation in psychology). *Nordisk Psykologi, 38*, 27-40.

Moustgaard, I.K. (1987). Psychological observation and description. *Psykologisk Laboratorium*. University of Copenhagen (stencil).

Sabra, A.J. (1971). The astronomical origins of Ibn-al-Haytham's concept of experiment. In: *Actes du XIIe Congrès International d'Histoire des Sciences, Vol. 3A*, pp. 133-136, Paris.

Teigen, K.H. (1981-83). *Psykologiens Historie* (The history of psychology). Bergen: Sigma.

Private thinking: Towards a theory
of therapeutic action in context [1]

Ole Dreier

I shall present some preliminary general considerations from an on-going empirical research project. It is based on the fundamental categories of the historical paradigm of "Critical Psychology" (e.g. Holzkamp, 1983) which developed out of the "cultural-historical" school in Soviet psychology, notably the work of A. N. Leontiev (Leontiev, 1981). The project is directed at conceptualising an important area of professional psychological activity: clinical practice, in a broad sense of the term. The results of the project will serve as guidelines for practitioners, reflecting upon limitations, problems, and contradictions of their current practice, and interested in determining possibilities for developing it.

Like all occupational activity, clinical practice is a specific, societally defined activity with a historically definite subject matter, goals, tasks, means, and conditions of work. Any individual practitioner acts under definite financial, legal, institutional conditions, at a particular location in a societal structure of health care. His actions contribute accordingly to the realisation of societal goals. His conditions present themselves to him as a constellation of meanings, indicating what can be done in relation to them.

Societal conditions not only embody objectified, generalised human experiences. They also constitute a definite societal constellation of meanings, referring to and connected in an overall societal structure. Individual subjects may relate to these constellations of meaning in various, alternative ways. Their actions are not fully determined by them. Fundamentally, a given constellation of meanings constitutes a definite - more or less restricted or extended - scope of action possibilities. In order to appropriate, utilise, and extend these possibilities, an individual must develop a functional, subjective action potency.

Cognitive processes are one functional aspect of that action potency. These processes develop as an aspect of the functional prerequisites of action

---

[1] A revised and extended version of this article, entitled "Denkweisen über Therapie", was published in Forum Kritische Psychologie 22, 1988, 42-67.

potency. Accordingly, a therapist develops his personal thinking as a functional aspect of his action potency in relationship to his occupational scope of possibilities. His personal thinking is a mental reflection on the experiences from his practice. It deals with his subjective way of relating to his social scope of action possibilities.

Nobody carries out this cognitive processing totally on their own though. The societally developed constellations of meaning already embody what they are thought out for, and what must be thought while utilising them. In other words, such experiences already exist in objectified, societally organised forms in the conditions and social relations, and are reflected in linguistic forms. We call them objective forms of thinking and language. An individual uses these objective forms of thinking to develop his personal thinking. He may, of course, at some points, arrive at notions different from those of the objective forms of thinking. He may even partially refrain from or neglect the endeavour of appropriating them. Besides, they are more comprehensive than what he can hold. So, his personal thinking remains a particular and partial mode of thinking. Just as the objective forms of thinking, his thinking may be queried for its contents of knowledge and for its functionality, being a particular, subjective answer to his scope of possibilities.

In our analysis of therapeutic thinking on this categorial basis we shall, at first, focus on some widespread notions about therapy. To individual therapists such conceptions are objectively existing forms of thinking and language which they use in various ways to process their own experiences. We shall query their practical functionality for thinking about therapeutic action, recognising at the same time that most of these notions arose precisely out of a reflection on practical therapeutic experiences.

1. Restrictions on Action in Existing Forms of Thinking

To begin with we notice a striking gap between the typical contents of therapeutic conceptions and our statements about therapy as being a specific societal practice carried out by professional subjects in definite occupational contexts: Typically, existing conceptions merely deal with clients' problems and with the immediate interactions between clients and their therapist. The therapist's actions in this immediate interaction are conceived of as an application of specific techniques. The therapist-subject is seen as a personification of these techniques and their underlying theories - also in the case where definite personality characteristics are considered to be his essential therapeutic tools. In any case, his actions are motivated and legitimated solely by the problems of the client. Everything falls back upon the client; anything else would appear to be an error, intruding upon the "real practice of therapy".

Let us put this contradiction in a different way: Everybody, probably, agrees that therapeutic action is a case of professional, societal action, and that its meanings and implications are determined within a societal constellation of actions. This is particularly so if they are reminded that even acting individually and in private is a special form of societal action and does not take place outside of society on an asocietal basis. Nevertheless, all this is not included in the typical forms of therapeutic thinking which are, on the contrary, conceived to be asocietal and abstractly (e.g. immediately and purely) individual. How then, can this form of thinking direct societally mediated action? The gap is now defined as a contradiction between forms of action and forms of thinking, and we can propose the hypothesis that this contradiction is the basic reason why it has not been possible to determine scientifically the meaning and effects of therapeutic action.

An interpretative mode of thinking (Holzkamp, 1983) is characteristic of therapeutic cognition and its existing conceptual forms. It is concerned merely with immediate interactions and personality characteristics and has obvious weaknesses. They are documented e.g. in the difficulties of assessing its truth-value and of choosing among a host of possible alternative interpretations of even the same case. An interpretative mode of thinking seems unable to establish a viable connection between theory and practice and, thus, legitimate scientifically the profession of therapy. In the following we shall specify some of its restrictions and contradictions, starting with its narrower forms and proceeding to the more extended modes of thinking which these contradictions demonstrate to be necessary in practice.

Furthermore, we shall point out that these restricted modes of thinking result from and legitimate definite, restrictive modes of coping by therapists within their societal forms of practice.

1a. Thinking in Predictions and Plans

We start with the notion that the therapist should be able to predict his therapeutic processes and outcomes on the basis of a preconceived plan or diagnosis.

Most therapists readily admit that their concrete practice does not work that way and that they have to transcend or abandon this form of thinking in their everyday practice. It presupposes that it were possible for them to unequivocally define a point of departure (problem, diagnosis) and a goal (solution, health), and hence to precisely determine the necessary means of proceeding from the one to the other. Theoretical conceptions are thus regarded as mere "cookbooks", consisting of ready-made solutions to already known, general problems. This stands contrary to the goal of therapeutic actions which must, essentially, be to support the development of something new and so far unknown which cannot possibly have been part of the premises of the prediction. In order that such general diagnostic categories or plans could become directly applicable, the therapist would have to be able to subsume his individual cases under these categories. Contrary to this essentialist notion (Jensen, 1987), in his practice the therapist will encounter many cases that are not readily subsumable. He will have to "adapt" his plans to his individual cases and, still, realise that the same procedures lead to different effects in different cases and in different contexts of action.

Thinking about these facts within this general notion, the therapist must either come to the conclusion that they are due to unessential, external circumstances, or to errors in the way in which he handles his cases. Assuming the notion were true, his therapeutic procedures would be mere routine-operations of carrying out a plan to its successful solution. On the one hand, his everyday practice then appears very unskilled. On the other hand, it becomes clear to him that a number of analytical tasks during the actual process of therapeutic change fall outside of the scope of this general notion and are left over to his private experiences and understanding (Dreier, 1985a). He gets no conceptional support for this thinking, and yet he may feel that often he misses important aspects and possibilities of case-work if he neglects it. Consequently, the therapist is thrown back upon his private, subjective processes of interpretation while constructing, modifying, and even applying his plans.

Furthermore, the therapist does not dispose over the practical conditions that might make it possible for him to predict what might happen in the course of the therapy and in the client's life. Nor does his client for that matter, even if he did, in fact, loyally try to execute his therapist's plans. The therapist might then, on the one hand, consider that very endeavour futile, and on the other, feel to be more acutely in need of means of control over his practice. This dilemma may make hirr 'ck to his notions about predictability - inspite of the fact that he knows they do not work reliably.

His clients may, on the one hand, welcome his intention to execute and control plans as a sign of professionalism, efficiency, and neutrality, as well as a taking-over of responsibility for the solution of their problems in relation to which they themselves feel powerless. On the other hand, his clients may react to the execution of his plan with various forms of resistance, withdrawal, reinterpretation, intermission, termination, etc. In such and other ways, the therapist is inevitably involved more closely in the relationship and into the conflicting interactional process. Once again, these theories give him no support in thinking about such difficulties. They rather tend to interpret these difficulties as an error on his part and to suggest to him a legitimate position of withdrawal and rescue from the strains of such precarious involvements.

Summing up, we can say that although these notions do not reflect the realities of everyday, therapeutic thinking and action, they not only are applied, but play an important role in the evaluation and self-evaluation of individual therapists: "You/I should have been able to foresee this or that." But they do so for societal reasons which these theories do not include and reflect: Their application is determined by a societal interest in having control over and professional responsibility on behalf of clients. Therapists may use such notions to make "precise" reports about their practice as a kind of cover against such pressures. But they must also, in part, take over this responsibility and control. They may do so the more easily, the "sicker" they believe their clients to be. And they may consider it to be their task to transfer a similar mode of "self-control" to their clients.

1b. Thinking in Action

It is becoming increasingly apparent in many professional disciplines that professional actions and outcomes, in fact, cannot be directly derived and predicted from general theories (e.g. Schön, 1983). Instead, various notions about heuristic strategies and reflection in action are advanced. They bring us closer to the everyday realities of thinking and action. The incompleteness and necessary modifications of interpretations, following problem-changes in the course of therapy, can be reflected. Therapeutic thinking can no longer be reflected merely as a process of solving problems, but as a developing interchange between aspects of definition and resolution of problems. Accordingly, the therapist can get more conceptional support regarding the complexity of his analytical tasks and many of its "microprocesses".

On the other hand, the notion of thinking in action essentially is a more resigned and defensive version of the notion of prediction and plan. It is still committed to the same basic claims and ideals. It merely realises them more modestly, less distinctly, and, therefore, cannot supply the same amount of outside legitimation, relief from strain, etc. The notion of thinking in action does remain somewhat vague - not because of the complexity of the matter, but because of its limited scope. It is no mere coincidence that it comes close to notions about therapy as a craft or an art. Those two forms of activity are, precisely, not put on a scientific form. They remain at a level of practical, instead of theoretical knowledge.

The notion about the relationship between theory and practice, inherent in such theories about thinking in action, is of a peculiar, limited nature, compared to what must be aimed at in a practice based on a scientific discipline. These theories about thinking in action do bring cognition and action closer together. But they take too little notice of the nature of their peculiar subject matter and of the context in which thinking in action occurs. Action and cognition are merely conceived of on the basis of their individual, subjective pole and must, therefore, appear abstract.

Of course, in reality the therapist is not confronted with a thing to be worked at, but with one or more thinking and acting individual subjects. So he is not the only one to do all the thinking. Nor is he responsible for and in control of everything. Therapeutic constellations and goals of action, tasks and processes of thinking are defined in supra-individual interactions. Indeed, no theory about a purely individual, cognitive form of processing and anticipation of actions can serve as an adequate, general model of human thinking and action. The meaning of an individual's actions and the nature and scope of his tasks and possibilities are no purely individual matter.

In the predominant notions about thinking in action, however, concrete client subjects and contexts appear as external factors to be arbitrarily implanted into an abstract model of purely individual thinking. Thus client actions unpredictably intrude upon therapist thinking, setting new tasks, demanding modifications of interpretations, etc. In that way, the therapist is exposed to uncontrollable events. Again and again he looses the internal directedness of his thinking, if he has not given it up altogether.

He may comfort himself by referring to the fact that notions about a permanently imcomplete and modifiable everyday thinking confirm such difficulties and make them appear unsurmountable. However, staying within the boundaries of such notions implies maintaining and increasing interpretative difficulties as well as neglecting the clients' cognitive contributions. It entails corresponding restrictions on action, forms of isolation and control, resistance and conflict, etc.

1c. Thinking in Interaction

The two notions treated so far - i.e. thinking in predictions and plans and thinking in action - have one restricting and conflicting feature in common: They both conceive of therapeutic thinking in practice as the therapist's thinking about his client. Supposedly, the client simply takes over the "reason" of his therapist. There seems to be but one centre of thinking (Mehan, 1984, p.

63) and but one version of "reason" present. In this sense we are dealing with issues of control and responsibility. Presumably, the therapist is located at a position outside and above the client and their shared context, from where he affects the client.

Whenever the therapist, contrary to this, wants to "come closer" on more "equal terms" of shared control and responsibility, and to include and utilise the client's thinking and action as a therapeutic device, he must consider both persons and their context. The most immediate version of this is the therapeutic session or encounter. The therapist, then, must recognise that this immediate therapeutic process is an inter-subjective phenomenon. Individual action and thinking in the session are part of an inter-individual process. Experience of and knowledge about the problem at hand are socially distributed across participants and across time (Mehan, 1984, p. 64). Nobody holds it all, not even he.

That is why one essential task is to collect and connect this experience and knowledge. It becomes an important task for the therapist to develop hypothetical constructs about internal connections in the problems. In so doing he uses his prior theoretical knowledge and experience to construct a theory about this problem, about this case.

That, however, is not to be confused with the therapist doing all the thinking and knowing it all. It may easily, willingly or not, lead him back into a position of sole responsibility and control, trying to hold together and to pull all the threads. Indeed, that would entail acting contrary to an important aspect of the whole therapeutic endeavour: By means of therapy clients are to develop their notions about the internal connections in their problems; they are the ones to judge their concrete validity and usefulness and to carry out the changes in their lives.

In accordance with that, it becomes the therapist's task to use his knowledge and experiences in such a way that he contributes to the support, guidance, and structuring of this movement. He is to contribute to the regulation of an intersubjective processing in the session, in such a way that connections can be seen and actualised, steps and goals formulated, and that clients become able to independently change, analyse, and communicate about problems with other people related to them.

All this does not imply the installation of a prohibition of thinking upon the therapist. It means that the therapist must learn to think differently and to use his thinking co-operatively in order that clients develop their consciousness about their problems and in order that he, in turn, can modify and develop his notions about the case. It requires of him to distinguish between his own thinking about the case and their thinking about it, about the therapeutic relationship, and even about himself and his actions.

Trying to do so he will, once more, be confronted with the fact that it simply does not work that way. He is faced with the difficulty that he and his clients do not agree concerning all these issues. And if this is the case, on which or who's grounds is he then to proceed? The disagreements among them might even be essentially connected with the conflicts for which the clients are in treatment. Therefore, the therapist cannot simply set them aside and e.g. work on the premises of his own immediate interpretations. He has to deal directly with these disagreements if he seriously wants to acknowledge the objectives of the therapeutic enterprise.

We shall not go into an analysis of clients here (cf. Dreier, 1980; in press). We shall merely point out that the eventual confusion of two parties into one centre of interpretation is determined by the meaning of such conflicts for the therapist in his occupational context. That may lead him in the direction of keeping his thoughts to himself, of being the chief judge, or of executing a monopoly of interpretation.

What is more, we must recognise that the idea of dealing with only one client is an untenable abstraction: Most often there are several clients immediately involved in the same case, and no single client lives entirely on his own outside society. So we do not have two centres, but several, at different levels, and the disagreement or conflict between therapist and client is but a special case of conflict and disagreement among all persons somehow involved. Who is right then, and how can we generalise about this (Dreier, in press)?

These conflicts are based upon differences of interests and possibilities as pursued in the societal reality of the parties involved. In order to come to understand his clients, the therapist must, therefore, transcend the boundaries of the immediate interaction.

The same holds true for his coming to understand the clients' actions within the session, their point of view upon the meaning of the whole therapeutic arrangement and upon his actions. The meaning of what goes on in the immediate interaction cannot be understood on the basis of the dialogue by itself. If interpretations - understood as hypothetical assumptions about connections in a case - are constructed merely on the basis of what appears in the immediate interaction, speculative short-circuits of more comprehensive connections will be inferred. At the level of the immediate dialogue itself, many phenomena remain in principle unequivocal. What constitutes adequate and effective therapeutic means cannot be determined on the basis of the dialogue alone. To try to discover the secret of therapeutic effects in some details of the immediate interaction is a dead end of practice and research. Of course, details may have an important meaning, but which meaning they do have must be determined on a more comprehensive basis.

1d. Thinking about the Client and His Life-context

At this point, most therapists will agree that the necessary conceptual extension for a theory of therapeutic thinking and action would be to consider the clients' extra-therapeutic life-context and its connections to what takes place within the immediate, therapeutic interaction. Some would claim, though, that all this already is included in the form of the topics of the dialogue. And they are right that it is, of course, talked about, etc. A lot of common professional and lay experiences inevitably are made about these inter-relationships.

Nevertheless, as with the previous level of the immediate encounter, they are not systematically included in existing conceptions. To recognise the meaning of the extra-therapeutic circumstances therefore also is left over to the therapist's own supplementary, arbitrary, private thinking. He might, e.g., interpret particular events within the immediate interaction on the basis of his own assumptions/knowledge about certain "external events" and the like. But since these inter-relationsships are systematically and conceptually undetermined, there is an overwhelming danger that he makes false, short-circuited interpretations about them, as well as about events and reactions within the therapeutic session. The therapist's evaluation of already realised therapeutic actions becomes beset by uncertainties too. All this has widespread disorienting consequences on his therapeutic thinking and action.

It is, indeed, surprising that so little is known about these connections, in a practice which proclaims to be so interested in the life and welfare of its clients. Yet, many therapists and researchers admit that the inter-relationships between everyday life and therapeutic sessions virtually are an unexplored aspect of therapeutic activity and effects. What is more, it is beset by methodological inadequacies and controversies: Either one seems only to be interested in the impact of therapy upon clients' everyday living as a kind of measure of therapeutic effects, in which case the inter-relationship is explored as a one-way affair with the therapeutic session conceived of as the centre and only agent. Or one explores the extra-therapeutic conditions as determinants of therapeutic outcome, again reducing the inter-relationship to a one-way affair, only this time seen from the other side. In neither way is the inter-relationship studied as such (cf. Dreier, in prep.).

We contend that the meaning of therapeutic actions and means, as well as of the whole therapeutic endeavour for a given client, must be determined on the basis of this inter-relationship. Their impact is mediated within the clients' life-context, and the "centre of gravity" normally lies outside of the sessions, in the clients' everyday life-context.

Since the clients' problems, conflicts, goals and tasks of therapy originate outside, so does its meaning and perspective. In order to take this into account, the prevailing interpretative mode of thinking about therapeutic processes within the immediate interaction must be extended to a more comprehensive mode of thinking (Holzkamp, 1983) by means of which the societal mediation of clients' conflicts, as well as of the meaning of their therapy is being comprehended. A theory about therapeutic thinking must be able to reproduce the objective, societal mediation of its immediate actions. If it fails to do so, its conceptions will be untenable in practice.

In fact, only when transcending the boundaries of what is immediately present and, in principle, sensuously observable or interpretable through empathy and the like, does the potential of specifically human thinking unfold. Only then is it not restricted to theorise about sensuous appearances and formalise their characteristics.

We are, therefore, arguing for a study of the scope of clients' possibilities in their life-context, in order that assumptions about the inter-relationships with their therapy must not remain speculative. Generalisations about the meaning of therapeutic actions and means must be based upon generalisations about problematic, individual scopes of possibilities in their life-context and about the adequate, therapeutic means by which they can be extended in the direction of transcending existing conflicts therein (Dreier, 1980; in press). In this way, we construct theories about definite types of scopes of possibilities and the adequate, typical means of extending them (Holzkamp, 1983, ch. 9).

Therapists will then be able to utilise systematically the concrete scope of possibilities of a particular case in their thinking and action. No more will they have to adhere to some pre-given conceptional forms of thinking as a kind of abstract norm for what supposedly is correct therapeutic behaviour under all concrete circumstances (Dreier, 1986). Therapeutic thinking and action must be generalised accordingly. That is the only way to systematically and constructively utilise the fund of practical, therapeutic experiences as an experiential basis and, thus, really connect experiences and theories.

1e. Thinking about Profession in Context

A conceptual extension into the clients' scopes of possibilities remains one-sided, however: It does not lead the therapist to determine his own occupational scope of action possibilities and its relation to the clients' scope. We only reach the level of a theory about professional, therapeutic action and thinking when the professional subject's own scope of possibilities is included. The therapist's own thinking and action also should not merely be interpreted within his immediate interaction with his client, but comprehended in its institutionally formed constellation of actions (Dreier, 1988; Dreier et al., 1988). Until then we are left with a theory about a practice without any professional aspect. That kind of theorising prolongs the present crisis of professionalism, instead of contributing to overcome it. What professional therapeutic competence, forms of action and directions of development reasonably may mean, must be defined to its agents and clients as well as to the rest of society.

The therapist's personal thinking must reflect his participation in his institution's realisation of objective, societal goals and the particular, societal meaning of his contributions thereto. Indeed, in order to be able to determine the meaning of his own actions and to fully utilise his own scope of possibilities, the professional subject must comprehend the objective, institutional constellation of meanings within which the meaning of his contributions and the scope of his possibilities are defined. Neither his possibilities, nor the meaning of his actions are immediately given to him. They must be thought out - by working himself into the constellation of meanings, reflecting upon his possibilities and upon his ways of relating to them.

The therapist's tasks and the criteria of their fulfilment are (in part) determined within these constellations, at various levels of the institution, even when he carries them out alone. Co-operation is primarily an objective, societal feature and only secondarily a matter of joint or individual action. It reaches into the forms of inter-institutional co-operation and societal health care.

Scopes of possibilities are institutionally organised, distributed and individually appropriated in some way or other. That includes definite procedures of decision making and treatment of cases as well. Cases are treated in accordance with institutional scopes of possibilities. Forms of case-work are made to fit within these scopes; of course, since one can only do what is possible. Other institutions influence these matters, at different levels of institutional activity, and according to the location of the institution at hand within a (more or less clear-cut) inter-institutional structure. In other words, institutions intersect, in various ways, and at several levels. They do so indirectly or directly within the institution at hand. Frequently conflicting interests are represented. Professional personal thinking, then, must be a functional aspect of a subjective action potency in relation to such constellations.

Institutional constellations render the use of definite procedures and means functional to professional subjects. Such procedures and means may be explicitly institutionalised and prescribed or merely informally chosen by the subjects within their scopes, filling them out in particular ways, often contra-dictory to prescriptions. For that reason, therapists need to generalise and theorise about these constellations and scopes of professional possibilities, in-cluding the strategies they apply to cope with them, utilise them in their case-work - and extend them. They need to systematically reflect upon how they use institutional and inter-institutional constellations in order to extend the scope of their case-work, organise adequate forms of co-operation, and widen their individual scopes into other levels.

Conversely, they need to comprehend how these constellations restrict the scope of their case-work, whether, where, and why they yield and change directions, reinterpret the case accordingly, feel subjectively strained by it, avoid certain conflicts, bring a case to a certain or sudden "solution" in order to avoid certain conflicts and be able to proceed "peacefully" and in time to another, etc., etc. They also need to reflect upon the conditions, reasons, and impacts of individual professional withdrawal as a peculiar, restricted, conflict-laden form of objective co-operation. They need to understand how such with-drawals eventually may lead them to stop thinking about other levels of case-work than those realisable "in private" and to install corresponding, person-alised modes of thinking about their work.

Finally, they need to reflect upon the meaning of definite, institutional constellations for client needs and in relation to client contexts. After all, such insights enable them to specify directions of institutional change in the interest of improving the service of client needs.

Following the directions advocated here, we may construct a theory about the inter-relationships between the professional's and the clients' scopes of possibilities. It may be reflected theoretically how each party relates to his own scope and to that of the others and how they thereby create a definite meaning and scope for the treatment undertaken.

Common professional experiences about all this, of course, exist in abundance, based upon local institutional relationships and endeavours. What constitutes adequate forms of concrete action and thinking must vary according to such local particularities. However, all such experiences are left over to private thinking as well. In particular, no conceptional support is given for linking them to the immediate case-work. They are processed unsystematically. In that way a lot of already made experiences are wasted, instead of being useful for others. Generalisations about action and thinking in definite types of pro-fessional socio-material scopes of possibilities are needed in order to lift insti-tutional scopes out of a state of apparently absolute, local diversity. As long as they remain there, attempts at theoretical thinking about institutional, profes-sional action rather take the form of contraposing institutional diversities with abstract generalities about e.g. "cognitive processes". Hence, abstract paradigms of cognitivism may introduce themselves to be "applied upon" individual contexts. That thinking always takes place in and deals with particular scopes of action is then no longer recognised to be a fundamental, general feature of human thinking.

The preceding arguments make it obvious that there are definite, societal experiences and interests of an often conflicting nature behind the objective, institutional structures of health care (i.e. their objective, socio-material constellations of meaning). Current forms, standards, procedures, and routines have resulted out of earlier compromises. They remain as they are or change and develop depending upon the current constellation of conflicting forces. It would, therefore, be a mistake to consider current routines as some kind of permanent feature or even determinant of institutional action and thinking. Nor are they simply neutral means of effectivity representing general human interests and experiences of getting the work done in everybody's interest. Using them inevitably implies becoming involved in particular ways in the compromise of interests which lies behind them, and in the pursuit of the societal goals for which they were developed. Their concrete meaning will be determined through the particular constellation of actions for which they are being used.

1f. Thinking about Development in Practice

Standards and routines thus reflect experiences about definite ways of handling conflicts within present forms, i.e. suggested modes of institutional and individual coping within the contradictions of everyday activity scopes. But they also are of a socio-historical nature (Jensen, 1987). They originated and were elaborated out of attempts at coping with problems confronted within specific, historical scopes of possibilities. Indeed, they were (in part) means of extending those scopes and of filling out new ones. They are, therefore, based upon experiences about such problems, possibilities and restrictions, and about the conflicting interests that lie behind them. And those experiences and standard procedures were mainly made by the professionals themselves.

In order to comprehend current modes of action and thinking, therapists and researchers, therefore, have to transcend present forms of everyday activity. Current problems, tasks, goals, conditions, means, and forms of action and thinking must be reflected in a socio-historical theory about therapeutic practice. The present scopes of possibilities of this developing practice arose out of the realisation of concrete possibilities, interests, and reasons by the professionals involved.

An adequate theory about therapeutic practice must be a theory about this development. Its fundamental categories and empirical generalisations must reflect the internal connections of such processes in a general form. In that way research explores the dynamics and processes of development and becomes a means of supporting further development, by producing means to analyse its concrete contradictions and possibilities. This brings the subject matter, activity, means, and goals of research into general accordance with those of therapeutic practice itself as a specific form of support to particular forms of contradictory processes of client development. The means, i.e. methods, of scientific as well as of therapeutic action must be adequate to support the extension of professionals' and clients' subjective scopes of possibilities - by generalising individual examples of such processes into empirical types. Obviously definite, societally mediated interests not only lie behind the kind of therapeutic means to be used, but also behind the scientific ones. They are adequate for a definite kind of goal and in conflict with another.

Exploring concrete, practical contradictions and possibilities in the way outlined here also makes it obvious that existing professional, institutional contexts are not totally objectively determined. Professional agents participate in their determination, elaboration, and change. It is, therefore, important to study systematically the scopes and strategies of action which professionals use in developing their practice, as well as to study the forms of thinking they thereby apply.

Within the area of therapeutic practice, the task of analysing and developing it does, in fact, in a peculiar way fall back upon the professionals themselves. Very little is done at an overall societal level to develop an adequate policy and plan for it (Dreier, 1988; Dreier et al., 1988). By the typical mixture of power and anarchy that prevails in our form of societal relations and politics of health care, such scopes do exist in surprising measures. Their realisation does, of course, confront professionals with the societal conflicts lying behind the compromises of current practice.

But that already is the case if they just stay within present forms. The restrictions and conflicts inherent in these forms create various kinds of "derived problems" for their participants, such as restricted practical results, conflicts, waist of resources, uncontrollable and unpredictable oscillations of scopes. It is exactly those concrete problems which motivate professionals' attempts at changing present scopes. Indeed, because of the preeminence of various forms of institutional contradictions and immediate conflict, institutions cannot even fulfil their societal objectives if their participants were to keep strictly to their prescribed rules. They would in many respects break down.

If we study existing institutional contexts as a set of conditions determining their participants' actions, we produce a kind of knowledge which not only does not comprehend the very processes of change, but depicts the agents to be controllable by definite conditions. We would produce yet another example of "a science of control over others" (Holzkamp, 1983, ch. 9). Our studies would focus on the influence of definite conditions upon their behaviour and subjective state, as well as on their ways of executing predetermined and repetitive tasks (i.e. the routines). We would come up with a theory about peoples' activities within given scopes and forms, stipulating those scopes as their absolute and unqueried premises of action.

To depict what repeats itself - and to restrict oneself to doing so for methodological reasons - primarily leads to studies about modes of reproduction of given forms, about the present empirical distribution of different unchanging forms, about the mechanisms of their restriction - instead of about the general and specific dynamics of their development. When the present forms change, such repetitions are changed, put out of force, disappear. They do, then, reflect present restrictions, i.e. what keeps things as they are. They can give us knowledge about processes within given limits, about coping strategies, subjective involvements, etc. internal to them. But they cannot give us any orientation as to their development, nor any historical perspective concerning their emergence and transcendence - even though their results may have been intended to appeal for change.

They also tend to split up the issue of determinism. On the one hand, some studies are based upon notions about total objective determination depicted in processes repeating themselves. On the other hand, other studies merely focus on "subjective constructions" undertaken ad lib, i.e. without touching the objective "boundaries" or considering the meaning of the given scopes for the subjective premises of these internal constructions. They do not explore the historically changeable relationship between being determined by and disposing over relevant conditions, according to the scope of possibilities at hand. Out of this arises the gap, we mentioned initially, between what is done in practice, i.e. actual scopes and forms of action, and what is reflected in the conceptions about it, i.e. the prevailing forms of thinking.

2.   The Functionality of Different Modes of Thinking for Professional Action in Context

Returning to our initial problem about the gap between forms of therapist action and thinking, at first, we must conclude from our line of arguments that to transfer and apply forms of thinking, developed for more restricted forms of action, directly onto changed and extended forms of action will lead precisely to a gap, a contradiction between the two. This gap is, in part, of a historical kind, due to the fact that a systematic theorising about the experiences from practical developments is lacking. Whenever restricted forms of thinking are applied directly to more extended scopes of action, they will, however, disorient and split up this practice "from within". They will lead to restricted realisations of present scopes and confuse their reflection and evaluation. It is noteworthy, in this respect, that among many practitioners the "ideal notion" about "what therapy really is" remains the private practice "behind closed doors", classically developed by Freud for a more restricted form of action (Dreier, 1985b).

Referring to the initial presentation of our conceptual position, we must also point to the importance of distinguishing between
a) the objective forms of thinking existing as cognitive implications of the objective, socio-material constellations of meaning and
b) the objective forms of thinking existing in conceptualised, in part written form as products of subjective processing of experiences about action in relation to the objective constellations of meanings.

The latter forms contain distinct ideological elements and presuppositions about their subject matter. But individuals cannot think totally without them. They must use them to mediate with their objective constellations of meaning. Their personal thinking will, therefore, be led off the track. As a result, their thinking will be characterised by restrictions, ruptures, gaps, internal contradictions and short-circuits with which to cover them up. It will also contain elements of experiences about what is misinterpreted or not reflected at all in the conceptual forms. In that sense, individuals may in their personal thinking attempt to transcend the conceptual forms and develop their own personal conceptions which normally remain at a mainly private level.

On the other hand, a conceptual form of thinking need not be accurate in order to be subjectively functional in a peculiar, restricted way for personal thinking. In order to elaborate this claim, we proceed from the distinction between objective forms of thinking and personal thinking to another categorial distinction within the paradigm of Critical Psychology (Holzkamp, 1983). Concerning personal action and thinking we distinguish between two fundamental modes:
a) the extended mode of action with the comprehensive mode of thinking as its psychological, functional aspect and
b) the restricted mode of action combined with the interpretative mode of thinking.

The first mode is used by individual subjects whenever they try to extend their scopes of possibilities and subjective disposition over them. The latter mode is used whenever they refrain from that and arrange themselves within the given scope. The two modes are fundamental alternatives, leading in opposite directions and always presenting themselves to individuals irrespective of their specific conditions. The choice among them depends upon the experienced, subjective functionality of using the one or the other in the situation at hand.

The comprehensive mode of thinking leads in the direction of reflecting on the concrete societal mediation of individual possibilities. Such a reflection is necessary in order to realise their extension. The interpretative mode, on the other hand, brackets off this societal mediation, out of experienced personal risks, conflicts, lack of possibilities, i.e. the experienced dysfunctionality of attempting to realise a relevant extension of the present scope. For that reason, it is restricted to thinking about what goes on within immediate situations, and about the individual course of life as if it were fully determined by such immediate situations. It is, in other words, characterised by short-circuited connections. These proclaimed connections either depict individuals as mere "victims" of their immediate conditions or disregard the meaning of conditions for their life, thus considering their life merely to be determined by immediate interactions between the persons involved and by their personality characteristics. In both cases it renders relatively static notions about what goes on since they both disregard subjects' potentials for disposing over and changing their scopes.

We have treated various aspects of the interpretative mode of thinking in existing conceptions about therapeutic action. These conceptions are concerned with abstract, personalised processes, presumably without any context at all, or with interactions conceived merely within immediate situations, and with changing what people may arrange immediately among themselves. In a second step processes taking place outside these situations, at various levels in society, may be conceived of in the same way as personalised phenomena. The fundamental problem about this interpretative mode of thinking is that it does not focus on the possibilities for overcoming mediated contradictions and for extending relevant scopes. Instead and because of that, it tends to make further steps in a restricting direction functional (cf. the analysis of restrictive modes of thinking in social case-work by Bader, 1985).

Since the societal mediation of immediate scopes is real, however, the immediate situation cannot be understood and conceived within its own boundaries and on its own premises. One can never finish trying to understand what goes on interpretatively. The interpretations produced remain equivocal.

One is left with a feeling of not fully understanding, a feeling that some secrets must be hidden in the details of the situation or at the bottom of the partici- pants' souls. The restrictive mode of action and interpretative mode of thinking can, therefore, only be fundamentally understood in theoretical terms on the basis of the comprehensive mode of thinking.

There are definite societal interests behind the propagation of such forms of thinking. But there also are definite individual reasons for their acceptance and use. They consist in a subjectively experienced powerlessness and in an anticipation of the endangering conflicts which would arise if the individual tried to extend restricting scopes. In other words, the reasons for applying an interpretative mode are founded in the subjective experience that it would be dysfunctional to choose the extending alternative. This is why, conditions then appear as external, unchangeable "frames". Either these conditions appear to inflict upon the individual without his being able to control them and, hence, present themselves as mere disturbances and annoyances. Or the conditions present themselves as something to be subjectively reinterpreted in such a way that they can be disregarded as irrelevant for the individual's current mode of coping.

Existing conceptions about therapeutic action are suggested modes of relating to such conflicts and restrictions, under the subjective premise that it is impossible to overcome them - for the professional as well as for the client. To both of them, the "technicism" of prevailing conceptions is an attempt to increase the effectivity of influence and control under the premise of subject- ive powerlessness over relevant, societal conditions. In that way "self-control" is to be installed under otherwise uncontrollable conditions. Many clients even seek therapy as a particular way of solving their problems, precisely because they do not want their existing scopes queried, but want instead some solution to be found within them, in private.

In other words, restrictive conceptions become subjectively functional for the professional for many reasons and at many levels of their practice. The lack of adequate, clear-cut, and realisable societal goals, plans, co-operative structures, competences, etc. for therapeutic practice makes it difficult to give individual practice a direction and context of development. Existing forms of inter-institutional and institutional co-operation often are full of conflict. The partialisation of interests, combined with unsolved conflicts, leads each institu- tion to "close itself up" to more encompassing levels of co-operation and each of its members to "concentrate" on "their own" clients. Subjectively affected by all such kinds of partialisation of interests, it becomes difficult for them to find out how to determine and represent general interests and create joint activity. They easily become disappointed, resigned over others and/or themselves.

On that background professionals feel left to cope with their practices in primarily individual, more or less isolated or private forms. Individualised and personalised modes of action and thinking become subjectively functional to them. Structural and institutional responsibilities become individualised, personalised, and part of inter-institutional and inter-individual conflicts.

The individualisation of the subject matter of the health care structure (Helbig, 1986) is, so to speak, reproduced in a corresponding individualisation of its agents. This forces them to think and act in definite, individualistic and restrictive ways in order to "fulfil their responsibilities". Many therapists do not comprehend the possibilities, restrictions, strains, and conflicts of their case-work as being their "internal structure" of the structures of health care. Instead, they try to transcend these strains etc. by developing skills and techniques aimed at making them act more effectively within their niche of immediate case-work. Concentrating in this way on their clients, and forgetting the societal conflicts which lie behind their immediate practice, the ideology of therapeutic practice conducted in the service of clients' needs turns into a conversion of the real power structure transferred between clients and their institutionalised therapists. The "forgotten" power mostly is realised in those particular ways in which professionals apparently subsume themselves to the needs of their clients'. Therapists mix restrictions and fulfilments of client needs and interests in subtle unaccounted ways. Having "forgotten" about the societal mediation of possibilities and restrictions it appears as if they must be able to find a solution to peoples' problems no matter what the scope of their real possibilities may be.

It follows from all this that the restrictive mode of action and interpretative mode of thinking are not only functional under the definite conditions described. Being contradictory and based on contradictions, they are, at the same time, necessarily dysfunctional, in the sense that they actively bracket off and restrict possibilities, do not lead to a real transcendence of the relevant problems and entail peculiar forms of derived problems. As already indicated, personalised responsibility and guilt become an essential subjective strain on the people involved. This personalisation is consolidated by the lack of adequate conceptual support, and by the frequently personalising ideologies of the current conceptions. Problems of orientation and evaluation thereby become personal problems for the therapist (Dreier, 1987). Conflicts, strains, ambiguities, and restrictions of current practice turn into permanent, inexorable, misinterpreted realities.

Out of these straining consequences, subjective reasons for a shift of direction and for extending the subjective scope of possibilities in a more tenable way may arise, once more presenting the alternative of an extending mode of action and a comprehensive mode of thinking. Of course, this does not lead to a short-range solution to all relevant conflicts. It merely poses them in another perspective. But the way one relates to them certainly is not indifferent, neither for the agents of this professional practice, nor for its client subjects.

References

Bader, K. (1985). *Viel Frust und wenig Hilfe: Die Entmystifizierung sozialer Arbeit* (Much frustration and little help: The de-mystification of social work). Weinheim: Beltz.

Dreier, O. (1980). *Familiäres Sein und familiäres Bewusstsein: Therapeutische Analyse einer Arbeiterfamilie* (Family being and family consciousness: Therapeutic analysis of a working-class family) (Texte zur Kritischen Psychologie Bd. 11). Frankfurt/M: Campus.

Dreier, O. (1985a). Zum Verhältnis von psychologischer Therapie und Diagnostik (On the relationship between psychological therapy and diagnostics). In K.-H. Braun & K. Holzkamp (Eds.). *Subjektivität als Problem psychologischer Methodik* (Subjectivity as a problem of psychological methods) (pp. 232-246). Frankfurt/M: Campus

Dreier, O. (1985b). Grundfragen der Psychotherapie in der Psychoanalyse und in der Kritischen Psychologie (Fundamental issues of psychotherapy in psychoanalysis and in Critical Psychology). In K.-H. Braun et al. *Geschichte und Kritik der Psychoanalyse* (History and critique of psychoanalysis). Marburg: VA&G. Reprinted in *Udkast* 1987, vol. 15, 1, 3-30.

Dreier, O. (1986). Der Alltag der Therapeuten: Widersprüche und Entwicklungsmöglichkeiten (Everyday activity of therapists: contradictions and possibilities of development). *Verhaltenstherapie und psychosoziale Praxis*, 491-497.

Dreier, O. (1987). Zur Funktionsbestimmung von Supervision in der therapeutischen Arbeit (On determining the function of supervision in therapeutic work). In W. Maiers & M. Markard (Eds.). *Kritische Psychologie als Subjektwissenschaft: Klaus Holzkamp zum 60. Geburtstag* (Critical psychology as a science of the subject: For the 60th anniversary of Klaus Holzkamp) (pp. 44-56). Frankfurt/M: Campus.

Dreier, O. (1988). Der Psychologe als Subjekt therapeutischer Praxis (The Psychologist as Subject of Therapeutic Practice). In J. Dehler & K. Wetzel (Eds.). *Zum Verhältnis von Theorie und Praxis in der Psychologie.* (On the Relationship between Theory and Practice in Psychology) (pp. 113-138). Marburg: VA&G.

Dreier, O. (in press). Client interests and possibilities in psychotherapy. In W. Maiers & Ch. Tolman (Eds.). Critical psychology: Towards a science of the subject. In *Forum Kritische Psychologie 20*, 1987, 66-83.

Dreier, O. (in prep.). Re-Searching Therapeutic Activity. In S. Chaikin & J. Lave (Eds.). Situated Learning.

Dreier, O., M. Kleinmanns, M. Konitzer-Feddersen, H.-P. Michels & A.Raitola (1988). Die Bedeutung institutioneller Bedingungen psychologischer Praxis am Beispiel der Therapie (The Meaning of Institutional Conditions of Psychological Practice Exemplified by Therapy). In J. Dehler & K. Wetzel (Eds.). (pp.81-112).

Helbig, N. (1986). *Psychiatriereform und politisch-ökonomische Strukturkrise in der Bundesrepublik Deutschland* (Psychiatric reform and structural, political-economical crisis in the FRG). Marburg: VA&G.

Holzkamp, K. (1983). *Grundlegung der Psychologie* (Foundation of psychology). Frankfurt/M: Campus.

Jensen, U. J. (1987). *Practice and progress: Towards a theory of the modern health care system.* Oxford: Blackwell.

Leontiev, A. N. (1981). *Problems in the development of the mind.* Moscow: Progress.

Mehan, H. (1984). Institutional decision-making. In B. Rogoff & J. Lave (Eds.). *Everyday cognition: Its development in social context* (pp. 41-66). Cambridge: Harvard University Press.

Schön, D. A. (1983). *The reflective practitioner: How professionals think in action.* New York: Basic Books.

On conations, psychotherapy and the concrete understanding of persons

Lars Hem

Henrik Poulsen has in the last several years worked with the substantial problems connected with theoretical conceptualisations of human emotions and motivation. One of the results of this work has been an effort to re-vitalise the old concept of conation. His main points are presented in an article on conations in the Danish journal "Psyke & Logos" (Poulsen, 1986). I will present some of the arguments put forward in this article and discuss some of its implications.

Poulsen's article falls into three parts. In the first part there is a terminological discussion that outlines some of the conceptual problems connected with the notion of conations. Part of this discussion is concerned with the difficulties of translating the English word "conation" into Danish, and will only concern us here in so far as substantial conceptual problems are elucidated by it.

The second part consists of a critique of the way in which the concepts of drive and motivation have generally been used within the scientific psychology of our century. This critique is supplemented with an outline of the historical roots of the notion of conations in both Danish and international psychology.

In the third and main part of the article Poulsen outlines the torso of a general theoretical psychology, in which the relationship between cognitive and conative mentation furnishes the cornerstone in an understanding of the human psyche. This theory is supported by phylogenetic arguments in the tradition of Russian activity theory as formulated by Leontiev (1981). In his exposition of the conative psyche, which Poulsen conceives of as the specific mentation of mammals, the concept of conation is clarified. The elusiveness of the concept in the initital terminological discussions and in the critique of the concepts of drive and motivation evaporates somewhat; the notion of conation solidifies and acquires depth as a central concept in a general psychological theory through the discussion of the phylogenetic origins of this type of mentality.

The article ends with some concluding remarks on the role of conations in the specific human psyche, focusing on the relationship between cognition and conation in human mental life.

The article taken as a whole is somewhat unevenly written. It is in the final part that the exposition first becomes fluent and forceful. There are too many minor points addressed in the first two parts which distract attention from the central issue. On the other hand, the central thought in the last part is of a kind that probably requires a book in order to be fully convincing.

Conation is not a Danish or Scandinavian word, even if it can be used in a Danish text. It is an English word, but also in English it has an antique flavour, and it is certainly not part of the daily language. Websters Dictionary defines "conation" as "striving, that partly is manifested in willful actions and partly can be found in consciuosness as will or desire". In Drevers Dictionary of Psychology we are told that the literate meaning is "striving", but "... (conation is) used either as a general term, inclusive of all experienced mental activity, or as itself the experience of activity as an ultimate type of experience, and not infrequently with confusion of these two senses" (Drever, 1964). The Penguin English Dictionary tells us that "conation" as a philosophical term means "the faculty of striving and desiring" and as a psychological term means "mental activity" (Garmonsway, 1976). From this a foreigner can learn that also in English "conation" is a word without sharp edges and without an obvious and clearcut meaning.

However, despite the apparent limited linguistic appeal of the term, Poulsen recommends its use - also in Danish - for the concept he has in mind. And, as anybody who has discussed theoretical issues with Poulsen can testify, the term "conation" is used effortlessly and with precision in his reasoning. It does fill up a conceptual space that is difficult to cover with other words.

Poulsen mentions that "conation" is used in the literature from the 18th and 19th centuries as part of a description of the human mind - or soul - as consisting of the trinity of cognition, emotion and conation. This is a way of thinking in which conation is one of the basic concepts in a faculty psychology. Faculty psychology is the name given to a notion of the mind with roots in medieval and aristotelian thought, where the mind (and any other object) is understood when one knows what essential features are expressed by it. In faculty psychology the mind is conceived of as having three essential features or faculties, and one of them is conation. In this view a conation is an expression of that part of the mind or soul where striving and desire are located. When Poulsen regretfully rejects "striving" as a suitable term for the concept he has in mind, it is because striving "...primarily refers to conations that are part of acts or activities, while "striving" is less suitable as a term for conations (wishes for something, desires for something, resentment or disgust towards something) of the sort that specify how humans relate to parts of their world, but which are not part of actions or activities."(Poulsen 1986, p.289, my translation).

The concept Poulsen has in mind, and for which he suggests we use the term "conation", is thus a basic concept in a theory of the psyche, as basic as the concepts of cognition and perception. In the psychology of our century the phenomena referred to by such a concept, that is, human striving and desire, has mainly been described and explained with the concepts of "instincts" (up to about 1930), "drives" (up to about 1950) and "motivation" (still in use).

There is a certain conceptual development connected to this change of vocabulary, but in my view it is the stability of the conceptual content that is more striking. The different terms are located in the same place in the descriptions and in the chain of arguments. They refer to the same, somewhat unspecified connection of biological states with human experiences as an answer to the question "Why did he do that?". In attempting to answer this question, most academic psychologists in the twenties would consider which instincts were fulfilled by the act, in the forties one would be told which drives that, modified by learning, were behind the act, while the answer in the fifties and sixties would specify the motivation behind the acts.

In this terminological development there is also a certain conceptual development in the way biological terms are used in psychological theorising. By this I mean that "instincts" usually refer to inherited behavioural dispositions, "drives" to biologically rooted, but modifiable behavioural tendencies, and "motivation" to that which energises and goal-directs the behaviour. But this change in the conceptual content probably tells us more about the way psychologists in different ages customarily delineate their subject from biology, and of the sophistication of the biological science that is referred to, than it is a sign of a clarification of the theoretically central problem that our strivings and our desires - our conations - presents for a general psychology.

One of the reasons that McDougal's theory of instincts became so popular in the first ten to fifteen years after the publication of his "Introduction to Social Psychology" (McDougal, 1908), was that his concept of instinct had such a wide application and was therefore seemingly so useful. But McDougal's instincts involved a classification of supposedly biological dispositions that were *defined by their goals*. It was not a term referring to sharply defined inherited behavioural sequences, as is the case with the modern concept of instinctual behaviour used mainly by ethologists. McDougal's definition of an instinct goes like this: "We may then define an instinct as an inherited or innate psycho-physical disposition which determines its possessor to perceive, or pay attention to objects of a certain class, to experience an emotional excitement of a particular quality upon perceiving such an object, and to act in regard to it in a particular manner, or at least, to experience an impulse to such an action." (McDougal, 1908, quoted in E. Murray, 1964 p.5).

As an example of a more modern treatment of the same issue we can use Edward Murrays own definition of motivation from 1964. It goes like this: "...there is general agreement that a motive is an internal factor that arouses, directs and integrates a person's behaviour. It is not observed directly but inferred from his behaviour or simply assumed to exist in order to explain his behaviour." (Murray, 1964, p.7). In his further specification, Murray asserts that a motive usually is broken down into two components. The first is the internal process that goads a person into action and which is called a *drive*. Second, a motive is terminated by reaching a goal or obtaining a reward.

From a conceptual point of view the central notion embedded both in McDougal's concept of instinct from 1908 and Murray's concept of motivation from 1964, is the perceived need to connect a drive or disposition which is, in principle, defined in bodily terms with types of goals or objectives in the sorroundings. In both cases, the statement implied by the conceptual structure - that which makes the instinct or the motive an *explanation* of the behaviour - is that it is the disposition/drive that decides that the goal/object is a goal/object for the behaviour under consideration. And in both cases the inference made in reality is *from* the specific goal/object of the behaviour *to* the specific instinct, drive or motive that supposedly selects this as a goal. The description of the behaviour is thus the operational definition of the theoretical concept that explains the behaviour, wherefore a conceptual circularity has been created instead of an explanation. This became generally recognised in the twenties, after the scientific literature had seen an inflation in the number of proposed instincts, including, according to Murray, an "instinct to avoid eating apples from one's own orchard" (Murray, 1964, p.6).

The roots of this circularity are, as Poulsen (1980) pointed out in an article on "Motives and motivation" (Poulsen, 1980) that the assumed bodily definition of the drives is purely hypothetical. The different drives are in fact not precisely observable with biological tools of measurement. Whether one speaks of instincts, drives or motives, all these concepts refer to hypothetical biological processes which in the actual research practices are operationalised in phenomenological or behavioural terms.

And these different concepts fill the same space and are used on the same conceptual level in the chain of arguments that explain the observations of human behaviour. This indicates that the problems confronted are of a conceptual or philosophical nature. That is, the problems are concerned with how the concepts are derived and how the chain of arguments should be designed in order to serve as an explanation; they are not theoretical problems in an empirical science that can be clarified with more innovative or more meticulous empirical research.

It is this conceptual structure, this explanatory design where human acts are explained as behaviour goaded by internal drives that also select their own goals that Poulsen finds unsatisfactory. His suggestion is to revive the old concept of conation and redefine it to fit modern theoretical and empirical insights. A clear concept of conation will contribute to clarify our understanding of human striving and desire, and thereby serve a useful function as a basic concept in understanding human activity.

It is not only within academic psychology that one finds this circular conceptual structure in what constitutes a theoretical explanation of human behaviour or the human psyche. The classical Freudian concept of instincts has the same structure. Theoretical psychodynamic explanations of a person's behaviour and experience run into the same conceptual circularity when they are understood as descriptions of instinctual development - the fate of the drives. This is so even if the psychoanalytic notion of cathexis, and in the modern version, of object-relations, introduces the concrete history of the individual into the explanatory scheme. As George Klein (1976) has convincingly shown, the psychological theory that is in fact used in actual psychoanalytic practice is not the classical Freudian theory of instincts, but a wholly different one which Klein calls *clinical* theory. Klein's critique of the classical Freudian instinct theory is conducted partly along lines similar to those I have sketched here. And the main conceptual features that Klein attributes to the clinical psychoanalytic theory have similarities with features that Poulsen attributes to a Leontievian activity theory modified by the introduction of the conation concept. I shall return to this after a presentation of Poulsen's discussion of the concepts of drive and motivation in modern scientific psychology.

In the article under consideration, Poulsen conducts his critique of the psychological concepts of drive and motivation along three interconnected lines. The first of these is to remind us that the psychological concepts of drive and motivation were more acceptable to the early scientific psychologists for philosophical reasons, (for what Poulsen calls Cartesian-dualistic reasons).

The classical concept of conation is embedded in a notion of human acts, in which the intentions of the acting person are a necessary part of any description and understanding of his acts. That aspect of the conations that is described as "striving" presupposes a necessary connection between an act and the intentions expressed by it. But with a Cartesian dualism as the philosophical frame, which assumes a sharp distinction between that which is external and that which is internal, between mind and body, these are not the acts of a person, but rather the behaviour of an organism that is to be understood by a scientific psychology. It is human behaviour in the form of external movements that is the subject matter of a scientific psychology. Therefore, in the theoretical explanations of human behaviour, of these external movements, one cannot use concepts that refer to internal or mental phenomena, such as conations, without negating the Cartesian framework. When this Cartesian frame was expressed and reformulated in early behaviourism's program for a scientific psychology, the notion of internal states or words with mental references was abandoned as unscientific, because such internal states were not what the behaviourists called objectively observable. The behaviour of the human organism was thus understood as a result of material processes in the organism that in principle were open to objective observation, e.g. brain processes or hormonal processes, and these processes were then referred to, for example, as instincts or drives. But, as Poulsen remarks, to speak of drives as brain processes was generally without substance; unofficially and off the record drives were conceived of as intentional and meaningful and spoken of as if they were conations.

The Cartesian way of looking at things implies that the intention and the act, the drive and the behaviour, are treated as independent units. But human acts cannot be described without implying our intentions. Therefore, when the act has to be described as behaviour, and as such, independent of its conation or intention, the conative meaning of the act is displaced to the supposed drive or motive. When the drive or motive is then conceived of as explaining the behaviour, the aforementioned conceptual circularity arises. Those aspects of the act that specify it concretely - its conations, are abstracted away and reintroduced as an explanation in the form of a drive-concept. For example, "hunger" is labeled as the motive that explains eating behaviour. But in the classification of a specific act as "eating behaviour", the hunger is already assumed. Hunger or the desire for food is the conation that specifies the act of eating from all other acts (Poulsen, 1980, p. 296). The example is taken from Sutherland (1959), where the point is extensively argued.

Continuing along this line, Poulsen introduces his second point, which is, that even if academic psychologists did leave the term "conation" behind - or never carried it with them from philosophy when psychology was launched as an empirical science, the conceptual content survived as an unspoken meaning in major parts of what we now call motivational psychology, disguised under the term "drive". As Poulsen puts it: "The concept of drive has become the scientifically respectable term for psychologists to use when dealing with conations." (Poulsen, 1986, p. 294).

His third and last point is that as a consequence of the Cartesian way of thinking, the contemporary psychology of motivation tends to deal both with motives that are mental phenomena, *and* with motives that are non-mental phenomena, whereby categorically different phenomena are dealt with within the same theoretical frame as being of the same kind. The concept of conations, however, maintains a pure category of mental relationships to objects in the world.

Behind these points one can discern a conviction concerning the task of general psychology, that is, what kind of questions should a general psychology be able to answer? One can also, perhaps, discern a conviction concerning what kind of arguments, empirical or otherwise, that are of importance in a scientific endeavour to formulate these answers. According to Poulsen, the task of a general psychology is to develop concepts that can grasp the basic mental reflections of man's relationship to his surroundings - and to himself.

One of the main chains of argument involved in the development of the basic concepts of a general psychology is the demonstration of the phylogenetic roots of proposed concepts. Poulsen's more philosophically oriented arguments in his critique of the psychology of motivation are thus primarily setting the stage for the real arguments in favour of the concept of conation. The real arguments in any scientific endeavour have to be built on an empirical foundation. In general psychology, the history of the species, and what this history can tell us about how different mental capacities have developed phylogenetically, provides us with one of the inevitable empirical foundations for these theoretical concepts. Even if these concepts are formulated on a level of abstraction that has traditionally been the domain of philosophers, it is this empirical foundation that secures their status as concepts in an empirical science.

From this analysis of how the concepts of drive and motivation are used and misused within academic psychology, and from the conclusion that the old philosophical and pre-scientific concept of conations has been the real notion in the shadows behind the conceptual circularities of the concepts of drive and motivation, comes a need for conceptual clarification. But, as Poulsen notes, merely clarifying the concepts with sharper definitions is not enough. Such an excercise would only end in formalities, unless these definitions have their roots in facts. And, it should be added, the relevant facts must be of a kind that are as general as the concepts one is trying to sharpen. This is the reason why Poulsen turns his attention to the phylogenetic development of conative mentation, with the intention of locating its origins in the history of the species.

He performs this location by describing how a conative psyche in mammals develops from appetent-behaviour in what he calls the "instinctual psyche", that which Leontiev labels the "sensory psyche". The instinctual psyche is characterised by a mentation where releaser-stimuli in the surroundings elicit standardised patterns of behaviour. In contrast, active striving in order to make an impact on the surroundings characterises the conative psyche, that which Leontiev calls the perceptive psyche.

In the instinctual psyche there is only a sensory registration of that which elicits responses, and thus no mentation either of the animals own capacities or of relationships in the world. In the conative psyche, on the other hand, there is a mentation both of the animals' own capacities and of relationships in the world. It is the relevance of the objects for the animal that is reflected mentally, and it is reflected as conative activities, as something that shall be attacked, escaped from, investigated etc.

Conative mentation also has the characteristics of primitive cognition, Poulsen maintains, in so far as the conative activities, the striving of the animal, can be more or less adequate under the particular circumstances. And the main point here is that this adequacy is tested through the impact of the animal's activity on the world. The conative mental reflection - the mentation of the environment's relevance for the animal in terms of activity - thus implies a rudimentary knowledge of the reality. And this is a knowledge that is continually tested by the impact of the animal's activity on the environment.

It thus makes no sense to talk of perception or cogniton in animals phylogenetically prior to the conative psyche, and on this phylogenetic level (which, as we remember, Leontiev calls the perceptual) the cognition is always embedded in conations. The perception of animals on this level is always a mental reflection in terms of striving. One could add, reminded of Mammen's (1983) distinction between perceptual sense-categories and selective-categories, that these perceptions in terms of striving are always actual, they are sense-categories. This is so even if elements of a specific and historical mental reflection, a mentation in selective-categories, perhaps can be traced among higher-order mammals in the form of habits. A certain kind of food is preferred to the exclusion of another, a certain path is perceived as easy, because of the specific history of the individual.

The foundation of the specific human psyche is the societal way of living and the human language. According to Poulsen, the important point here is firstly, that the language makes it possible to maintain a mental reflection independently of the activities; and secondly, that the societal mode of production has both conation-free cognitions and cognition-free conations as one of its concequences.

The meaning Poulsen attributes to the notions of conation-free cognition and cognition-free conation makes it clearer how the concept of conation can serve as a basic concept in a general psychology, that is, in a theoretical understanding of human mental life. Societal production implies that tools and other objects for common use are produced, and these acquire what Poulsen labels "general meaning" (Leontiev uses the term "objective meaning" or "objective significance" for the same notion (1981, p. 226f)). The mental reflection of such objects acquire, according to Poulsen, the characteristics of conation-free cognition. By this he means that a tool, as part of the productive equipment of my society, can have a meaning for the sustainment of my life, and I can perceive it as such without any need on my part to relate to the tool. I might have knowledge of its inevitability in the sustainment of my life, and yet, there might be no striving, attraction or repulsion connected to this knowledge.

The same holds for another sort of conation-free cognition, namely, the mental reflection of what Poulsen calls the "personal significance of objects", and what Leontiev calls "personal sense" (1981, p. 229f). Of these Poulsen states: "..(it is a mental reflection) of the factual relevance of objects to the needs of the individual (its meaning as dangerous or safe, healthy or unhealthy, hostile or friendly for just this person) (1986, p. 314)". To characterise the personal significance of objects as conation-free cognition looks a little surprising at first for those who are acquainted with Leontiev's way of thinking, and who are therefore used to treating his concept of "personal sense" as the conceptual tool available when one is interested in individual history and in an indivual's strivings and desires. One had rather expected some reflections on how the significance of the personal history among humans requires an understanding of the mental reflection of this significance, which might have been an argument for a concept of personal conations or the like in order to grasp this significance in its specificity.

The reason for having a distinct concept for the personal significance of objects, and for distinguishing it from the general concept of conation by characterising it as a conation-free cognition, might be that such personal significance of objects can function as motives for acts. Such motives are a specific human form of motivation, in contrast to the internal drive motivations based on bodily needs and incentives, both of which we share with other mammals. When the personal significance of an object functions as a motive for an act, it serves as an explanation of the specific individual's intention. And, if we remember the criticism against calling hunger a motive for eating, it is necessary to avoid the conation concept in defining "the personal significance of an object", if we shall avoid circularity when we use the concept to explain individual intentions with specific acts.

And an explanation of individual intentions - an explanation that can be formulated in the terms of general psychology, is *the* problem that has to be solved, if the theories of general psychology shall ever be able to contribute to the practical work of phychologists with individuals, in psychotherapy, councelling and assessment.

As an introduction to his presentation of George Klein's interpretation of Freudian theory in the article "Leontiev, the concept of mental reflection and general psychology", Poulsen writes: "If scientific psychology has to be a general psychology in the sense that it only addresses those aspects of mental life that are common for humans and specific to the species, it entails unacceptable consequences. Scientific psychology then becomes a science that refuses to attend to the mental functions in their concrete forms, as they are actually manifested in specific societies and in specific individuals. Scientific psychology then has no role to play in the understanding of mental functions as they are manifested in the practical work of psychologists, and the research in applied psychology will of necessity deal with phenomena that are too specific to be of interest for scientific psychology. If scientific psychology is conceived of as a general psychology that has as its subject matter those attributes of the mind that are common to the species, then scientific psychology looses its pracical interest, and practical psychology becomes unscientific" (Poulsen, 1982, p. 170). According to Poulsen, George Klein's suggestion of a specific clinical theory of psychoanalysis illustrates along which lines a general psychology has to develop, in order to avoid this dismal fate.

In his book "Psychoanalytic Theory" from 1976, George Klein points out that what is traditionally called "theory" in psychoanalysis, the metapsychology with its theory of the instincts and the topical and structural model of the mind based on this theory, is seldom used to explain or to understand the issues brought forward by the patient in analysis. In the clinical practice there is another theory at work, a theory that designates certain past events as significant for the patient and provides a framework for interpreting the meaning of the patient's contemporary experience in light of these past events. This, what Klein calls the clinical theory of psychoanalysis, is a theory of how the sensual aspect of events and relationships in our personal history takes on a significance and contributes to our sense of identity and gives shape to our emotional life. It is a theory that enables us to understand how present relationships are signified and distorted by past experiences, and how these experiences motivate a painful or dreadful perception of present circumstances.

This clinical theory maintains that for humans it is the personal significance of events and relationships that is of importance in creating our motives, and it maintains that sensual relationships are the basic signifiers, the foundation of the significance of all later events. It is this theory that gives meaning to the therapist's efforts during clinical sessions, where he sees his task as one in which he shall be of help to the patient in his struggle to be aware of the personal significance he consciously or unconsciously attributes to the events and relationships in his life.

In Poulsen's terminology, the clinical theory outlined by Klein focuses on man's specific mental capacity to be motivated by the personal significance of objects and events. This personal significance is reflected mentally as conation-free cognitions and it is because of this they can serve as motives for the person's attitudes and acts - as objects for the persons conations. Corresponding with this theoretical framework is the therapist's effort to help his patient become conscious or aware of the personal significance and meaning of certain issues which influence his emotional state, and how these personally significant issues can be reinterpreted. This reinterpretation is one that is, in principle, substantiated in psychoanalysis by the emotionally corrective experience of the transference relationship, or by functionally similar events in experiential psychotherapy.

There is a similarity in conceptual structure between Poulsen's modified activity theory and the modified psychoanalysis George Klein presents as the clinical theory. It is a promising fact that the two authors arrive at this conceptual structure from very different points of departure and through different chains of argument. Poulsen's conceptualisation is derived from his work with the general psychology of Leontiev. It is the twin problem of getting a theoretical grasp on human motivation and of applying the abstract categories of activity theory to the practical understanding of persons that is Poulsen's issue, and which he suggests can be solved by reintroducing a modern version of the old concept of conation within Leontiev's conceptual frame. While the problem that occupies Klein is the sterility of classical Freudian metapsychology and its lack of connectedness both to clinical practice and to the general psychology of our time. His solution is to derive from clinical practice the concepts that are actually serving as the clinician's theoretical frame. The clinical theory outlined by Klein is in practice both guiding the therapist's concrete perception of his patients and his understanding of how the patient has become what he is. It is in itself a strong argument for the conceptualisations arrived at, that in spite of the considerable difference in their points of departure and frames of reference, Klein and Poulsen formulate solutions to the question of how human motivation should be understood theoretically that are strikingly similar.

One can perhaps say, as Poulsen suggests, that the clinical theory of George Klein is a practical psychology that can be given a general theoretical underpinning by the activity theory modified by Poulsen with the use of the conation concept. Or, to put it another way, that the modified acitivity theory can serve as that general theoretical framework for the clinical theory in psychoanalysis that is needed when Freud's metapsychology has to be discarded.

If, in understanding human motivation, a conceptual bridge is to be built over the gap between the phylogenetic arguments of general psychology and the concrete experiences of therapy, the concepts developed by Poulsen and Klein, each from his own side of the crevice, look like the tools needed to build it with.

References

Drever, J. (1964). *A dictionary of psychology*. London: Penguin.

Garmonsway, G.N. (1976). *The Penguin English dictionary*, London: Penguin.

Klein, G.S. (1976). *Psychoanalytic theory*. New York: International Universities Press.

Leontiev, A.N. (1981). *Problems of the development of the mind*. Moscow: Progress Publishers.

Mammen, J. (1983). *Den menneskelige sans*. (The human sense). Copenhagen: Dansk psykologisk Forlag.

McDougall, W. (1908). *An introduction to social psychology*. New York: Barnes and Nobles.

Murray, E.J. (1964). *Motivation and emotion*. New Jersey: Prentice Hall.

Poulsen, H. (1982). Motiver og motivation (Motives and motivation). *Psyke & Logos, 1*, 179-211.

Poulsen, H. (1982). Leontiev, genspejlingbegrebet og almenpsykologien. (Leontiev, the concept of mental reflection and general psychology). *Psyke & Logos, 3*, 161-175.

Poulsen, H. (1986). Om konationer (On conations). *Psyke & Logos, 7*, 289-317.

Sutherland, N.S. (1959). Motives as explanations. *Mind, 68*, 145-159.

Webster's Third International Dictionary, 1968. Springfield, MA: Merriam Co.

Henrik Poulsen's published works, 1960 - 1989

Poulsen, H. (1960). Perceptuel konstans. (Perceptual constancy). In *Festskrift i anledning af E. Tranekjær Rasmussens 60 årsdag* (pp. 109-112). Copenhagen.

Poulsen, H. (1961). Intellektualistiske erfaringsteorier i amerikansk perceptionspsykologi. (Intellectualistic theories of knowledge in American psychology of perception). *Nordisk Psykologi, 13*, 257-272.

Poulsen, H. (1963). Den behavioristiske og den fænomenologiske tradition i perceptionspsykologien. (The behaviouristic and phenomenological tradition in the psychology of perception). *Nordisk Psykologi, 15*, 168-182.

Poulsen, H. (1964). Nogle problemer vedrørende klassifikationsafgørelser på grundlag af psykologiske tests, symptomer, anamnetiske data eller lignende. (Some problems concerning classificatory decisions based on psychological tests, symptomws, anamnetic data and the like). *Nordisk Psykologi, 16*, 17-24.

Poulsen, H. (1964). En ramme-model til beskrivelse af adfærdens hierarkiske organisation. (A frame model for the description of the hierarchical organisation of behavior). *Nordisk Psykologi, 16*, 125-131.

Poulsen, H. (1964). En teoretisk diskussion af nogle sider af intelligensbegrebet. (A theoretical discussion of some aspects of the concept of intelligence). *Nordisk Psykologi, 16*, 259-272.

Poulsen, H. (1969). *Om psykonbegrebet.* (On the concept of the "psychon"). Aarhus: Akademisk Boghandel.

Poulsen, H. (1972). *Kognitiv struktur.* (Cognitive structure). Copenhagen: Akademisk Forlag. (Thesis of Habilitation).

Poulsen, H. (1973). *Begreber og begrebsdannelse.* (Concepts and the formation of concepts). Copenhagen: Berlingske Forlag.

Poulsen, H. (1976). Materialistic conceptions of cognition, the principle of reinforcement, and Skinnerian behavior therapy. *Scandinavian Journal of Psychology, 18*, 1-9.

Poulsen, H. (1978). Psykologisk Institut, 1968-78. (The Institute of Psychology, University of Aarhus, 1968-78). In G. Albeck (Ed.), Aarhus Universitet, 1928-78. Aarhus.

Poulsen, H. (1980). Antropologi og livskvalitet. (Anthropology and quality of life). In E. Petersen (Ed.), Livskvalitet - baggrund, begreber og måling, Vol. 1, *Psykologisk Skriftserie, Aarhus, 5*(2), 196-213, Institute of Psychology, University of Aarhus.

Poulsen, H. (1980). Motiver og motivation. (Motives and motivation). *Psyke & Logos, 1*(2), 179-211.

Poulsen, H. (1982). Leontjev, genspejlingsbegrebet og den almene psykologi. Kommentarer til artikler af Ole Dreier og Benny Karpatschof. (Leontiev, the concept of reflection, and general psychology. Comments on articles by Ole Dreier and Benny Karpatschof). *Psyke & Logos, 3*(1), 161-172.

Poulsen, H. (1983). Om "Den menneskelige sans". (About "The human sense"). *Psyke & Logos, 4*(2), 362-368.

Poulsen, H. (1985). Om redskabskonstruktion og menneskelig psyke. (On the construction of tools and the human psyche). In O. Fenger & S. Jørgensen (Eds.), *Skabelsen, udvikling, samfund. En forelæsningsrække* (pp. 49-55, 270). Acta Jutlandica LX. Samfundsvidenskabelig serie 16. Aarhus: Arkona.

Poulsen, H. (1986). Konationer. (Conations). *Psyke & Logos, 7*(2), 289-317.

Poulsen, H. (1989). *The concept of motive and need in Leontiev's distinction between activity and action.* In this volume.

Poulsen, H. (in prep.). Inner "mental" processes, or forms of relating to the world.

Poulsen, H. (in press). Forholdet mellem subjekt og objekt i dyrs og menneskers erkendelse. (The relation between subject and object in the cognition of animals and men). In S. Brock & P. Petersen (Eds.), *Dømmekraft.* Aarhus: Aarhus University Press.